Footsteps

The Cream of South Wiltshire Walks

edited by

John Chandler

First published in the United Kingdom in 2002 by
The Hobnob Press, PO Box 1838, East Knoyle, Salisbury SP3 6FA

British Library Cataloguing in Publication Data
A catalogue record for this book is available from the British Library.

ISBN 0-946418-10-1

Typeset in 10/12 pt ITC Officina Serif and Futura
Typesetting and origination by John Chandler
Printed in Great Britain by Salisbury Printing Company Ltd, Salisbury

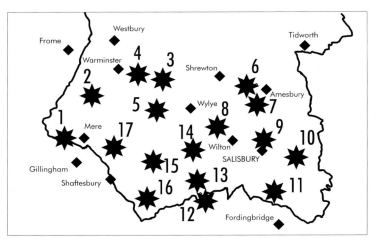

Approximate locations of the walks in relation to local towns and
villages

Contents

Introduction

The solitude and desolation of chalk downland, the timeless antiquity, the serenity of rivers in their wooded valleys, intimate villages of greensand and thatch, ancient churches, pubs and paths – walking in South Wiltshire cannot fail to invigorate and delight! This is a book by local writers and walkers who all know these landscapes well, and who have been exploring and studying them for many years. They were invited to choose and describe their favourite walks, and then to enthuse about their history, literature, geology, wildlife, archaeology – whatever is their particular interest. As editor I have tried to allow each contributor his or her idiosyncrasies, while imposing a certain degree of consistency. The arrangement is as follows.

Instructions are printed in bold type in numbered paragraphs, which correspond to the numbers on the accompanying sketch maps. These maps are schematic only, and walkers are strongly advised to refer to the relevant Ordnance Survey maps (preferably the Explorer 1:25,000 series, of which sheet number(s) are given in the heading to each walk). Between the instructions are paragraphs of description, photographs, and shaded boxes which give information about specific topics. There are also suggestions for further reading. Anyone walking in the countryside should respect it, shutting gates, leaving wildlife alone, dropping no litter, and keeping to public rights of way and permitted paths. The contributors and publisher believe that the details in this book are accurate as to rights of way (in 2002), but cannot accept responsibility for any errors or ambiguities.

I should like to thank all the contributors for their willing and friendly co-operation in producing this book, and in particular Ken Watts, who has not only read the whole work, but has also drawn the thumbnail map accompanying each walk. My grateful thanks too to Dave Cousins who has designed the striking cover.

John Chandler

1 An Infant River

Stourhead, White Sheet Hill and Mere

(6 miles/ 10km; can be extended to 9 miles/14km)

by Isobel Geddes   (OS Explorer 142, 143)

This circular walk begins in the wooded sandstones of the Wiltshire/ Somerset border at Stourhead, famous for its gardens landscaped in the 18th century. From Stourton, the path rises into the forest of Selwood, hunting ground of medieval kings, crossing the Six Wells Bottom, the source of the river Stour, which feeds a series of lakes in its valley here. Beyond, the path leads into ancient droveways over the Chalk downlands to White Sheet Hill. The Neolithic enclosure, Bronze Age barrows and Iron Age hillfort are testimony to the attractions of this place, with its wonderful views. A ridge of Chalk leads down to Mere where Long Hill, once the site of the town's castle, overlooks three counties. The return route runs between the outlying Chalk hills of Zeals Knoll and Beech Clump, back to Stourhead. There are good pubs and a cafe at Stourhead and even more facilities at Mere. The walk can be conveniently split into two sections: a downland walk to White Sheet Hill and Mere of about 6 miles (10 km) and a 3 mile (5km) circuit in Stourhead woods.

1 **Setting out from the car park for Stourhead (National Trust) and Stourton House Flower Garden (ST 779 340), avoid for the time being the National Trust Visitor Centre and the cafe; instead, turn left into the lane where you entered the car park and head down the hill.**

What with Stourhead Gardens, Stourhead House and Stourton House Flower Garden too, you may immediately be tempted to divert from this walk, as all three are worthy of inspection.

1

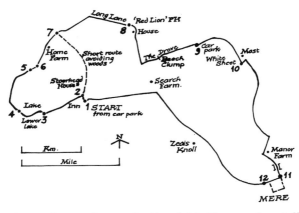

Well, perhaps afterwards . . . On the right, the grand castellated entrance gate to Stourhead House comes into view, more of a folly than a fortification. Note the dull greenish-grey sandstone of which it is built. This is from a rock formation known as the Upper Greensand; it looks greener when wet, and if you examine it carefully, you can see that as well as sand, it contains dark green specks of an iron mineral called glauconite, which gives the rock its colour. The mineral crystals form only in marine environments – so the sandstones underlying this woodland were laid down in ancient seas. This was 100 million years ago in the Cretaceous period. The builders of Stourton made use of this local stone as you will see.

2 **If you want to shorten the walk and miss out Stourhead woods (which can be very muddy after wet spells), turn**

Stourton church

right through the gateway and follow the footpath northwards (avoiding the drive to the house), which will bring you to a gate out on to a lane after 700m. Continue north up this lane for a further 600m and resume the route at point No. 7.

Further down the lane, on the left, a group of buildings includes the village hall, built as a war memorial, and the *Spread Eagle* Inn, which does good bar food (and is open all day). The delightful little church, set back from the road and blending into the landscape, is of late medieval date, with pierced parapets and embattled tower. It contains Hoare family tombs and monuments – the builders and owners of Stourhead. Below the church, across the road, after a row of cottages stands a tall monument. This is the old Bristol Cross, perhaps somewhat out of place here overlooking the lake.

THE BRISTOL CROSS   It was erected in 1373 at the main crossroads in the heart of medieval Bristol. Elaborately traceried, with statues of kings and queens in its niches, at 13 metres high it used to sway in the wind. There it stood for 350 years until it was removed for fear of its falling. It was at first placed in a safer and more convenient positon by Bristol cathedral, where it remained for another 30 years. But after a period of storage in the cathedral cloisters, in 1768 it was given by the Dean of Bristol to Henry Hoare, the owner of Stourhead and creator of the gardens in the 1740s.

The lake is surrounded by a wonderful variety of mature trees. In spring, as the first buds burst, magnolias and camellias bloom, later to be followed by an amazing collection of rhododenrons and azaleas. The latter thrive, as do bluebells, on the acid sandstone soils. In autumn, the changing colours of the leaves give a magnificent array of golds and russets, yellows and reds, scattered among the sculptural evergreens.

A little further along, the lane goes under another folly, known as the Rock Arch. It is made of giant irregular chunks of dark, glassy-looking chert; this occurs naturally within the local Upper Greensand. Chert is a form of silica (as is sand), originally derived from the dissolved remains of sponges with siliceous skeletons, living on the Cretaceous sea floor.

3 After the Rock Arch, turn right immediately, down a track beside a lake.

The Rock Arch, Stourhead

The lake on the left is a lower lake, below the garden lake (which is obscured by bushes on the right).The track runs between two of the series of lakes created by damming the valley of the infant River Stour. By this pond is an old water wheel and pumphouse, dating from 1920. The wheel powered a pump raising water from the springs here up to a reservoir in the woods where there was sufficient head of water to supply the estate.While on the subject of water holding, it is perhaps

STOURHEAD GARDENS The English 'Landscaped Garden' at its best, it was created by Henry Hoare II in the 18th century. The grounds are laid out to appear natural and informal but with carefully placed follies among ornamental trees, to be viewed from specific vantage points, as was the fashion of the time. The design was based on the landscape paintings of Claude Lorraine, depicting an allegory of the journey of Aeneas after the fall of Troy, as described in Virgil's *Aeneid*. With this in mind, the path around the lake should be followed in an anticlockwise direction! Whichever way you go, the vistas of trees, shrubs and water are lovely throughout the year, but particularly in Spring and Autumn. The first rhododendrons were introduced by Richard Colt Hoare, his nephew and heir, in 1791; since then the collection has grown and grown to produce a wonderful blaze of colour in season. This treasure of the National Trust is open daily throughout the year.

interesting to note that all Stourhead's lakes are sited on the thick impermeable clay formation beneath the Upper Greensand, known as the Gault Clay. It is found at the surface in the valley bottoms here and allows the lakes to retain water.

Water wheel, Stourhead

4 Continue along the track, passing the junction signposted 'Park Hill' on the right and passing Beech Cottage on the hillside. Shortly after the cottage, after crossing a stile/gate across the track, turn right uphill on a footpath leading upwards into the woods (ST 766 341), leaving the main track below. This path can be muddy and slippery – be prepared! It goes over the hill, crossing three broader tracks – but is always marked by arrows labelled 'Stour Valley Way'. Finally, it descends into Six Wells Bottom, where it emerges from the wood to pass between the upper two ponds.

Six Wells Bottom is the source of the River Stour, and up the valley to the left St Peter's Pump is visible, placed there in 1768, over the Stour's first spring. The pump was removed from Bristol in 1766 – just two years before the estate acquired Bristol's High Cross as well!

5 Having continued up the other side of this valley and back into the woods, take the track signposted 'Stourhead House'. However, after a few metres, turn left up the hill, along a footpath which brings you to a stile where two footpaths cross by Terrace Lodge.

These woods are part of the deer park created in the 15th century by Sir John Stourton, treasurer to Henry VI. He was granted a licence to enclose one thousand acres of the king's private hunting forest – the Forest of Selwood. Only patches of woodland survive from this medieval royal forest, which once extended from Somerset to Warminster and Shaftesbury.

6 At the crossing of the footpaths at Terrace Lodge (to the left after the stile), carry on straight ahead, following the sign to 'White Sheet'. Follow the field boundary to the left beyond the lodge, until a stile is encountered. Once over this stile, follow the path along the fence (on the right) to Home Farm, which is not far ahead. Skirt around the farm along the track to the road.

Terrace Lodge is on 'The Terrace', the north-eastern boundary of the Stourhead deer park. At this point you leave the woods for the open farmland below the Chalk downs. To the right stands the Obelisk, another landscape feature erected in 1746 as part of the 18th-century re-designing of the grounds. The lower part of the structure is local Greensand, but the upper part is limestone – a stronger stone, perhaps used in its rebuilding in the 19th century.

7 At this point (ST 775 352) if you want to cut short the walk and return to the car park at Stourhead, turn right along the lane for 600 metres, and go through the gates on the right, topped with interesting wooden knobs, on to a public footpath (not signposted) where the lane bends sharply left. You pass in front of Stourhead House (a discreet distance away) and emerge at the gatehouse almost opposite the car park, which you will find if you turn left then right shortly after.
   If you plan to continue to White Sheet Hill, cross the lane at the Home Farm entrance drive and go through the gate opposite with the fingerpost marked 'White Sheet'. Follow the path along the garden boundary, then straight across the field towards the line of trees marking Long Lane Drove. Go over the stile and turn right into the track, following it to the main road, opposite the *Red Lion* pub.

> STOURHEAD HOUSE The Lords of Stourton were
> dispossessed of their estate for supporting and housing
> Charles I during the Civil War. It was bought in 1717
> by the notable merchant banker Henry Hoare, who
> pulled down the medieval house and built a mansion in
> the grand neo-classical style of the 18th century. The
> architect was Colen Campbell, *the* designer of the day.
> Inside is fine Chippendale furniture and the walls are
> hung wth portraits and landscapes. The house (now
> owned by the Nationl Trust) is open from April to
> October, Saturday-Wednesday.

Long Lane Drove is part of an ancient track which was used from
medieval times to drive cattle from the Somerset Levels across
Wiltshire towards London. It is a sunken holloway, typical of
Greensand country, the banks awash with flowers according to
season: primroses, celandines, wood anemones and ground ivy;
followed by bluebells, red campion, comfrey and willowherb.

8 **The *Red Lion Inn* is open for lunches (a good variety
served from 12.00-1.50pm - last orders). A few metres
up the narrow lane beside the pub, turn right into the
entrance drive of a house. Go through the gate left of the
driveway, skirting around the property, following the path
along the field boundary (on the right) to another gate.
Beyond this, the path leads through yet another field with
mature trees, finally joining a track known as The Drove
(ST 788 346). Turn left here, either at the gate or stile and
up the track through another gate/stile, where reassuring
yellow arrows appear, on to the knoll called Beech Clump
for obvious reasons. Follow the path to the White Sheet Hill
escarpment.**

Above the Upper Greensand lies the Chalk – a thick formation of
fine white limestone, the deposits of tropical seas covering
England in late Cretaceous times around 80 million years ago. It
underlies all the downlands of southern England. Beech Clump
marks the ascent on to the Chalk and is the first of the many
outstanding viewpoints soon to be encountered. The clump has
two generations of beech, separated in age by perhaps 50 years.
There is a stone memorial to airmen whose plane crashed here in
1945. From the knoll you can see the route of the rest of the
walk. Left of Beech Clump is the isolated Zeals Knoll, then left
again is Long Hill above Mere, then further left still is the high
Chalk escarpment where the path ahead leads. Several rampart

banks of the Iron Age hillfort of White Sheet Castle are visible
to the right of the radio mast. The old chalk quarry which gave
the hill its name is to the left, below a Bronze Age round barrow
on the skyline. As you climb higher, the chalk ridges of Long
Knoll and Little Knoll come into view to the north. To the right
of the hillfort is the ridge this route will follow as it steps down
through successively lower levels of the Chalk towards Mere. The
fine mature beech trees ahead mark White Sheet Hill car park.

**9 At the White Sheet Hill car park, go over the stile at the
back corner, following the yellow arrow by the National
Trust sign. Head through the old quarry towards the hilltop
ridge and over the stile at the top of the quarry (another
yellow arrow). From here proceed to the round barrow and
then towards the radio mast and reservoir mound.**

The old quarry has a bit of whitish chalk still on the steepest
quarry face – it would have been much whiter when freshly
exposed. Looking back over and beyond Stourhead, Alfred's
Tower stands above the trees on the western horizon. Built in
1772, on the Wiltshire/ Somerset border, at 53 metres high, it is
reputed to be one of Britain's tallest follies. The views from the
top over Somerset are magnificent. This supposedly is where
King Alfred gathered his troops together,after emerging from
hiding in the Somerset Levels, before going on to defeat the
Danes at the Battle of Edington in 878 AD. As you climb to the
top of the hill notice the parallel 'sheep tracks' down on the
scarp. Otherwise known as terracettes, they are actually soil-
creep features, the result of downhill movement of soil over
thousands of years.
    Behind the prominent Bronze Age burial mound at the top of
the hill are less obvious Neolithic structures. There was a late
Stone Age causewayed camp here – probably a meeting place for
prehistoric markets and ceremonies 5,500 years ago. Short
lengths of bank and ditch can just be made out. Further on a
Bronze Age cross dyke ridge leads down from the top of the hill
– a mere 3-4,000 years old. Then you reach the hillfort dating
from the Iron Age, built 2,000 – 2,500 years ago. Its high
ramparts and deep ditches suggest a defensive function.
    This is an area with a natural chalk grassland flora, a nature
reserve. Typical plants include wild thyme, horseshoe vetch,
knapweed and orchids. Butterflies such as the Adonis and
Chalkhill Blues and a variety of snails thrive too. The chalk
provides the latter with an abundant supply of calcium
carbonate for their shells. There is, perhaps incongruously, a
Royal Observer Corps bunker also located here. The views reach

south to the claylands of the Blackmore Vale (the Stour valley) and the downs of Dorset. South-eastward, the Vale of Wardour cuts into the Chalk and even through the Greensand. The latter forms the flat-topped hills. As you look to the south-east, the Chalk of Cranborne Chase rises behind to the horizon. Beech Clump and Zeals Knoll now seem dwarfed in comparison.

10 **The aim now is to follow the ridge southwards: there is a stile beyond the triangulation point by the reservoir. Having crossed this stile, head for the back of the reservoir and over another 'stile' over the fence ahead to get on to the ridge-top. Follow the east side of this fence, descending all the time until a gate leads on to a track. Further on, past Manor Farm, there is a gate leading on to a lane. Turn left here (ST 809 331) in front of the farmhouse, then over the A303 road (a bridge) and into Mere (Manor Road).**

As you descend successive levels of the Chalk on the ridge dropping down to Mere, look back at the hillfort and its wonderful site. It is clear why it would appeal to the people of the Iron Age, who specialised in constructing such defences at intervals along the Chalk scarps, and indeed other prominent hills. Hillforts on the Greensand are less obvious as they always seem to be obscured by trees. By the time you reach Manor Farm, Casle Hill and Long Hill are looming up ahead, sheltering the small town of Mere. Notice the pond on the right, where water emerges from the lower levels of the Chalk.

11 **If it is time for refreshments, carry straight on into Mere. Manor Road leads to the main street. The *Old Ship Hotel* (to the right on the main road) does good lunches. To avoid Mere and continue the walk, turn right off Manor Road, taking the signposted footpath up steps to**

> MERE Though actually on the Chalk, this little town has the atmosphere of the Upper Greensand – the older buildings have a distinctive greenish-grey tinge: notable are the *Old Ship Hotel*, with a fine 18th-century iron sign, and the quaint clock tower in the centre of town. The 13th – 15th century St Michael's church is well worth a visit; its exquisite medieval carved wooden screens surrounding the chancel are outstanding. Mere Castle is no more; built on the hill-top in 1253 with six towers, it once dominated the town. Sadly it fell into ruin in the 15th century.

Castle Hill and Long Hill – opposite the first row of brick houses (on the left). If you go off to explore Mere, rather than retrace your steps to get back on the route, you can turn right past the *Old Ship Hotel*. Shortly after you will come to an antiques shop; beyond the shop an alley runs to the right leading upwards to a lane; on the opposite side, a path leads through a playground on to Castle Hill.

The *Old Ship Hotel*, Mere, built of Greensand

Castle Hill and Long Hill together form an outlying chalk ridge, preserved as such because its two summits are topped by a particularly hard band, known as the Melbourn Rock. Erosion by streams in the past have cut it off from the main escarpment of the downs. This vantage point affords views of three counties. A plinth atop Castle Hill conveniently points out the landmarks. You can see again the entrance to the Vale of Wardour, with flat-topped Greensand hills behind, such as that on which Shaftesbury is situated, a defensive site overlooking the Stour valley. The flat clay vale of the Stour lies to the south, on the other side of a fault running just south of Mere, which has brought clay against chalk and caused such a contrast in landscape north and south of the town.

12 **Below the plinth, to the west at a gate, the path splits in three. Take the middle way up along the ridge and down its western end on to a bridge over the**

> **THE MERE FAULT** You cannot fail to notice the abrupt change in the landscape to the south of Mere: the flat claylands of the Stour valley contrast sharply with the Chalk downs to the north. The reason for this is geological – a major fracture cuts the Earth's crust here, running in an east–west direction. The clays to the south are Jurassic in age (150 million years old). There was movement along it right through Jurassic time, when this area was covered by tropical seas on the margin of a continent being constantly stretched as the Atlantic Ocean slowly opened up. The tension produced cracks and resulted in constant subsidence of the sea floor over millions of years. Later the tension was replaced by compression as Africa pushed against Europe when the Alps were formed. This reversed the movement on the fault and the Jurassic clays were pushed up level with the Chalk.

A303 road. Head along a (muddy) track towards Zeals Knoll, standing ahead on the left. The path passes north-east of Zeals Knoll heading for Search Farm. Just before the farm, take the path to the left (ST 791 341), westwards towards the B3092 road, emerging opposite the turn-off to Stourhead. Cross the main road and you will find the Stourhead car park on the left, after Stourton House Flower garden.

Zeals Knoll is another outlying lump of Chalk cut off from the rest of the Chalk of Wiltshire over time, a more subdued knoll of just the lower levels of Chalk, again capped and thus preserved by the hard Melbourn Rock. The curious name Zeals comes from the Old English word *sealh* meaning sallow or willow, which is also present in the forest's name, Selwood. Before you get to the knoll, you will have evidence that the underlying rock is Greensand from the chunks of it lying around the field. Ahead, White Sheet Castle and Beech Clump dominate the vista and on the final leg of the route, there are further views of Castle Hill and Zeals Knoll, all the more satisfying for having been there.

Further Reading

Geddes, I. 2000, *Hidden Depths: Wiltshire's Geology and Landscapes.* (Ex Libris Press, Bradford-on -Avon).

Watts, K. 1998, *Exploring Historic Wiltshire: volume 2: South.* (Ex Libris Press, Bradford-on-Avon).

2 Dry Bones

Longbridge Deverill and Cold Kitchen Hill (8 miles / 12.8km)

by Nigel Vile   (OS Explorer 143)

Walking guidebooks all too often enthuse about rather undistinguished walks. In this case, every adjective in the outdoor writer's vocabulary would have to be used to do justice to what is a truly magnificent slice of landscape in a secluded corner of Wiltshire. A quiet byway and tranquil green lanes are merely the prelude to a stiff climb on to Whitecliff Down and Cold Kitchen Hill. The effort is worth every bead of perspiration, however, with views across the Upper Wylye Valley that are never less than impressive. This is an ancient landscape, with the Ordnance Survey recording mounds, tumuli and barrows at every turn. Such is the outlook from these lofty hilltops that a beacon was erected here in centuries past to warn of invasion and to celebrate victory in conflict. At journey's end, your steps will end up passing the George *in Longbridge Deverill, quite the perfect spot to rest and linger awhile following a walk that will remain long in the memory. Incidentally, given the open and exposed hilltops, with the potential for far-ranging views, you should consult a reliable weather forecast before setting out.*

1 Longbridge Deverill lies on the A350 road to Shaftesbury, just 3 miles south of Warminster. In the centre of the village, just by the *George Inn*, turn off the main road along the unclassified road signposted to Maiden Bradley. Park with consideration on the roadside in the vicinity of the inn (SU 868 408). Follow the Maiden Bradley road westward for 1km to Wing Farm (SU 858 406). Immediately before the drive leading into the farm complex, turn left along a narrow enclosed bridleway.

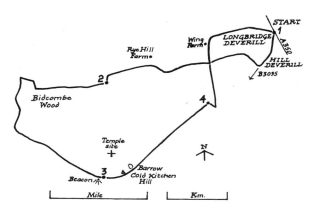

Follow this bridleway for 375m to a crossroads of tracks.
Turn right, and follow a wide grassy ride for 1km to its
junction with a farm track emerging on the right from Rye
Hill Farm (ST 849 402). Follow this track directly ahead to a
gateway, before continuing ahead across a narrow field.
Halfway across this field, keep on the track as it bears left
and then right into the adjoining field. Continue along this
track, the field boundary on the right, to the corner of the
field, and keep following this track as it bears left to follow
the end field boundary up to a gate. Immediately beyond
this gate, turn right and follow an ill-defined path
alongside a fence to a gate/stile (SU 842 398).

One commentator records that Longbridge Deverill 'does not
hang together well as a village from the point of view of layout'.
It is easy to understand these sentiments, with the village lying
astride the busy A350 which carries a steady stream of heavy
traffic to and from the south coast. There is no real focus to
Longbridge Deverill, merely a collection of elements that do not
blend together into a pleasing whole. The oldest part of the
village lies at its northern end, where the Thynne Almshouses
lie alongside St Peter and St Paul's Church, just above the River
Wylye. The almshouses, dating from 1655, owe their origins to
Sir James Thynne of nearby Longleat. With a focus of three
gables, each protecting a three-light transomed window, the
attractiveness of the almshouses is lost somewhat due to the
proximity of the main road.

The Norman church, with many later additions, again has
associations with the Thynne Family of Longleat. It is here that
we find the family chapel, housing the earthly remains of Sir
John Thynne the builder of Longleat House. The incongruity of
the church is epitomised by a Norman arcade and font, which
stands alongside carved and painted screens from 1921. These

13

The Beacon, Cold Kitchen Hill

screens were a gift from the vicar, the Reverend Brocklebank, as a 'thank offering to Almighty God for 50 years of manifold mercies'. The Reverend Brocklebank was also responsible for several windows of a rich and ornate design, one of which depicts the origins of Christianity in Britain, as well as the establishment of St Peter and St Paul's Church in Longbridge Deverill.

2 Follow the left edges of the next 2 fields alongside Bidcombe Wood for 1.25km. At the far side of the second field, beyond a gate, follow the left edge of the next field uphill through some trees until the fieldpath reaches a gate on the left-hand side (ST 828 398). Beyond this gate, follow a steep path uphill for 700m to the next gate at the exit from Bidcombe Wood. Beyond this gate, cross a hilltop field to the end field boundary, before turning left and following a hilltop fence across three fields on Whitecliff Down to a hilltop beacon. (SU 842 382). Below the beacon are fine views across the Upper Wylye Valley.

Historically, beacons were erected on prominent hilltops both to warn of danger and to signal seasons of national celebration. The Armada was signalled from here in July 1588, an event that was commemorated some 400 years later with the erection of the current beacon. Chains of light would spread throughout the kingdom, as flames would fan out from the Quantock Hills to the Mendips before heading east into Wiltshire. This is certainly an outstanding viewpoint, high above Kingston Deverill and Monkton Deverill, with views across the Wylye Valley towards King's Hill and Pen Hill. It is a lonely and secluded hilltop site, with the constant sound of the skylark filling the air in summer months.

3 **Just past this beacon, fork left along a signposted bridleway to reach the triangulation point on Cold Kitchen Hill, which stands at 257 metres above sea level. Continue walking in the same direction past the trig point to a long barrow, before walking in the same direction downhill to a tin barn (ST 849 386). Cross a track at this point to a gateway opposite, before following the right edge of the next field to the next gateway, just a short distance down the end field boundary from the corner of the field. Beyond this gate, cross a small hilltop paddock to the next gate, before continuing to a crosstrack. Beyond the gate ahead, head across to the far side of Brims Down – passing a copse on the right – to a point where a fence forms a corner. Keep ahead – a fence on the right – down to a handgate, before following the right edge of the next field down to a gate in its bottom right corner (SU 859 396).**

Cold Kitchen implies meatless bones, and could have associations with an extensive Romano-Celtic temple and cremation area, the site of which lies on the hillside to the north-west of the triangulation pillar. Many partially burnt Romano-Celtic brooches were found during excavations of the temple site, indicating the presence of a crematorium, with nearby Brimsdown Hill being further substantiating evidence, Brimsdown being a name associated with fire. This rural temple, built near the crossing point of the Roman roads running from Bath to Poole and Old Sarum to the lead mines on Mendip, possibly marked the border between the Durotriges to the south and the Belgae to the north.

From Cold Kitchen Hill, the views range in all directions. Cley Hill is visible to the north, Warminster to the north-east, Cow Down to the east, the Deverills lie below in the valley, and the isolated chalk hills of Long Knoll and Little Knoll lie to the west. The long barrow just below the triangulation pillar is 230 feet long and 8 feet in height. Referred to as *lang beorh* in a Saxon charter, this particular barrow has prominent side ditches, and dates back to 3,000 or 4,000 BC.

> ROMAN TEMPLES The main styles of Roman temple were the classical, the Romano-Celtic and the Mithraic. The classical temple was an elevated rectangular platform with a row of columns supporting a porch. The shrine was approached by a flight of steps, at the foot of which was an altar for public sacrifices. The Romano-Celtic temple consisted of a ground plan of two squares, one inside the other. The inner room was the shrine (*cella*) surrounded by a colonnaded wall and covered portico. The Mithraic temples were small rectangular buildings with a recess at one end where the altars were placed. The body of the temple was divided into three parts longitudinally. Just inside the entrance would be a small annexe screened off from the main part of the temple.

4 Cross this gate, and follow the track ahead for 75m to a junction. Turn sharp left at this point, and follow a bridleway for 750m to crossroads of tracks – the crossroads passed early on in the walk. Turn right, and follow this side track for 750m to its junction with the B3095 in Hill Deverill alongside some properties. The undulations in the field to the right at this junction mark the site of the medieval village of Hill Deverill (SU 867 402). Turn left along the B3095, pass John Hurd's Organic Watercress business and continue to the A350 in Longbridge Deverill. Turn left and pass the *George Inn*, before turning left into the Maiden Bradley road.

John Hurd is thought to be the only organic grower of watercress in the country. His 47 beds are fed every day with 3 million gallons of pure spring water pumped up from bore holes 120 feet down in the chalk. With favourable conditions, crops are grown continuously throughout the year, although a severe temperature drop can hinder growth. During the winter, John Hurd grows a French-American cross, like virtually all cress growers, but from May to September the main crop is an English variety. The English cress, with its pointed rather than round leaves, possesses a better flavour according to the experts! The watercress can be purchased direct from the packing sheds or from the nearby Deverill Trout Farm in Longbridge Deverill. This is another organic business which, in addition to trout reared in sparkling spring water, sells an interesting fish paté.

Further Reading

Wilson, Margaret, 1987, *Wiltshire Villages* (Ex Libris Press)
Woodruffe, Brian, 1982, *Wiltshire Villages* (Hale)
Wright, Geoffrey, 1988, *Roads and Trackways of Wessex* (Moorland Publishing)

LONG BARROWS As well as a knowledge of simple farming methods, polished flint implements and pottery, early Neolithic settlers brought with them the practice of burying some of their dead under long earthen barrows. Important members of ruling families were buried with accompanying rituals beneath the often broader eastern end of long barrows. The human remains were placed in an inner mausoleum with objects for the after-life, such as pottery bowls, broken sherds and flint implements. Earthen long barrows are common features of the rolling chalk downland of Wessex. These first prehistoric structures, situated in conspicuous positions on the slopes or brows of hills, are now thought to have been centre of religious practices, and burials were not the only reason for these impressive mounds.

3 On the Antiquarian Trail

Heytesbury, Chitterne, Upton Lovell and Knook (10.5 miles/ 17 km)

by Nick Cowen   (OS Explorer 143)

A challenging circular walk exposed to the elements on the southern perimeter of Salisbury Plain, with extensive horizons under huge and dramatic skies. Setting out from Heytesbury the route soon ascends the massive chalk plateau open and wild, but safely outside the military training area. Strewn across this unique and ecologically rich calcareous landscape are the visible prehistoric remains of many millennia of occupation which can be viewed along the way: Bronze Age burial sites, prehistoric field systems and the Knook Romano-British villages. Midway the walk descends to Chitterne where there is a pub (Kings Arms). The path then traces the course of the winterbourne Chitterne Brook, before rising up for more expansive views and antiquarian delights, and returning via Upton Lovell and Knook to Heytesbury. You will be walking in an area with virtually no cover from sun, wind or rain so, depending on the season, common sense precautions are essential.

1 Begin at Heytesbury (ST 927 426). Leave the village on the old A36, walking 500 metres east to meet its new route, and cross to its northern side. Continue on the pavement, bearing left with the Chitterne road (B390). After 100m take the first left up a tarmac lane (ST 936 425). At Bevin's Barn (ST 938 432) cross the new military road on to the grass, follow round the top of the coombe (Dunscombe) for a further 1km east to Willis's Field Barn.

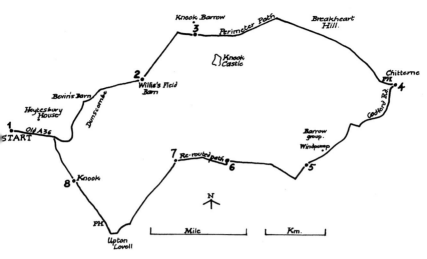

Cross between the new house and the paddock, and turn left at the stile.

Once you have climbed up around Dunscombe with your back to the Wylye Valley you can now look ahead across the vast area that is Salisbury Plain. Ignore if you can the concrete perimeter road, that seems to run coincidentally with the footpath on occasions for this first section, and ignore also any buildings, modern fields and fences, and even clumps of beech trees as these too are a modern introduction. The open, almost steppe-like plain that we are left with is the product of a huge-scale clearance of the so called 'wildwood' that had flourished across Britain since the post-glacial rises in temperature from about 8,000 BC onwards. Before the arrival of the Neolithic people in approximately 4,000 BC there was very little natural grassland, but using only stone as a cutting edge they began the systematic deforestation of the landscape. Progressively the tree-cleared areas were cultivated or grazed and here the succession of Bronze and Iron Age farmers would complete the process. Today we have a much clearer idea of the chronology of prehistory, but 200 years ago William Cunnington from Heytesbury began to explore the conspicuous burial mounds and settlement sites of these earlier cultures, riding out on the Upper Chalk with only murky and often inaccurate archaeological guidelines.

When I walked this route again in early April I was amazed at the number of cowslips among the springy grass turf, particularly at ST 943 434, between Bevin's Barn and Willis's Field Barn. I was also lucky that I neither heard nor encountered

Samuel Woodforde R.A. pinx.ᵗ   James Basire sculp.ᵗ

William Cunnington FSA, of Heytesbury: the frontispiece to Sir
Richard Colt Hoare's *Ancient history of south Wiltshire* (1812)

any military activity on the Plain, and spent the entire day (4
hours walking) in the company of skylarks, with a wonderful
ambient twinkling of endless song. I certainly saw buzzard,
lapwing and fieldfare, and you may even catch a glimpse of a
hen harrier if you are very fortunate. In the summer months
you will encounter a diversity of butterflies, perhaps common,
chalkhill or even Adonis blues, skippers large and small and
migrants also – Red Admiral or Painted Lady.

As you continue north-east towards the useful landmark of
Knook Barrow, there will inevitably be blocks of grazing sheep
somewhere in view. Today they are penned in with electric
fencing and are moved systematically, and the lonely roaming
vigil of the shepherd is now consigned to history along with the
Wiltshire woollen industry.

2 From the stile walk for 1km to a T-junction of new roads next to a clump of beech trees and continue straight ahead towards Knook Barrow for 300m on the grass. Meeting the unsurfaced track (ST 953 445), with an Imber Range Perimeter Path signpost, turn right, and keep on this track heading east.

'WILLIAM CUNNINGTON YOU MUST RIDE OUT OR DIE' This ultimatum was delivered by his doctor to a prosperous Heytesbury woollen merchant, who had been suffering from a disease which resulted in debilitating headaches and depression. William Cunnington (1754-1810), despite the lack of a formal classical education, was a thoughtful intelligent man who had already cultivated a dual interest in antiquarian and geological pursuits. In search of fresh air and exercise, and accompanied by his barrow-digging labourers, he set about the practical examination of the prehistoric sites in his neighbourhood. An important partnership and an unlikely friendship was to develop in 1803 between Cunnington the tradesman, and the aristocratic son of a wealthy banking family, Sir Richard Colt Hoare (1758-1838). It had become the Stourhead baronet's ambition to write *the* book on Wiltshire prehistory, and with Cunnington's agreement he organised and financed an extensive campaign of barrow 'opening'. In all some 465 burial mounds were excavated, but often, it has to be said by today's standards, rather hurriedly.

The barrow artefacts, once they had been illustrated, remained with William Cunnington on display in 'The Moss House', a rustic building in the grounds of his Heytesbury home, and many illustrious visitors signed the visitors' book. But for Colt Hoare the real treasure was the information gained from the evaluation of the work undertaken by William Cunnington in that last decade of his life; these letters and reports were woven into the text of the first volume of *Ancient Wiltshire*. Despite a glowing dedication in the front of the book to William Cunnington when it was first published in full in 1812, it is Colt Hoare's name that was embossed on the broad leather bindings of those sumptuous volumes that graced the shelves of the great private libraries and learned institutions of 19th-century England.

Items from the 'Stourhead Collection', as it became known, can be viewed at the Wiltshire Heritage Museum, Devizes, and are well worth the visit.

You have now joined the Imber Range Perimeter Path (IRPP), with its distinctive field gun logo on the signpost. The view from this track is as close as one can approach Knook Barrow and the less obvious Neolithic long barrow in the foreground. Under no circumstances should you venture off this track into the danger area. At this point there are spectacular views to the west of the prominent chalk hills around Warminster: Cley Hill in the distance, with Scratchbury the nearest, then Middle and Battlesbury Hills with their respective Iron Age hilltop fortifications.

A further 500m on, with the profile of the Iron Age Knook Camp visible in the near distance across the grass field to the right of the track, and the standing earthworks of the Romano-British village in the field to our left, you are now entering an area of once concentrated habitation. 'For on our bleakest hills', as Colt Hoare wrote, 'we find the luxuries of the Romans introduced into the British settlements, flues, hypocausts, stuccoed and painted walls, etc. etc'.

The benefits of life on the high ground with its thin soils must have outweighed the problems of living without a nearby source of water. Look out for the hump in the track that is part of a prehistoric ditch that may pre-date these settlements. There is another Romano-British village a bit further along the track on the right. If you look along the base of the long tree line of beech in front of you, at the far side of this field, you will be able to determine the broad and regular profile of the terracing of the individual earlier fields as they descend the slope.

3 Keeping to the track climb up from the dip, following the I.R.P.P. signs, to ST 969 448, and keeping the fenceline tight on your right-hand side, pass close by the top end of a long belt of trees. Continue on a steady descent for 2km to Chitterne. At the road (ST 987 439) turn left, then cross to walk on the right-hand side with only intermittent pavements. The *King's Arms* pub is on the left after 250m.

Gradually our route drops down to the village of Chitterne, and the track becomes more sunken with rising banks on either side. There is a partially obscured milestone on the right 350m from the bottom. It is difficult to read now but once indicated 'VIII to Warminster – XIV to Sarum'. Locally I have heard it referred to as the Bath Road.

4 From the *King's Arms* re-cross the road, and turn right on to the Codford road. After 1 km take a footpath on

the right (ST 984 431), cross Chitterne Brook, take the stile
on the left near the parish boundary stones and enter the
long field. Pass through the field gate near the windpump,
and across the next field to the lower left-hand side of a
belt of trees, go through a field gate and on to the tarmac
track.

A FEW PLAIN FACTS In 1897 the War Department
purchased 364 acres of land in Market Lavington. The
Salisbury Plain Training Area now occupies 94,000
acres.

The new perimeter road runs along the southern
and western fringes of the Plain and is 26 miles long,
6-9 metres wide and required an estimated 500,000
tons of imported stone to construct. It is designed to
take 60-ton tanks and is guaranteed for 60 years.

Before the decline of the Wiltshire woollen industry
travellers across the Plain were astonished by the many
huge flocks of sheep that they encountered. In 1724
while on his tour of England and Wales Daniel Defoe
observed 'Tis ordinary for these flocks to contain from
three to five thousand. . .'

Shimmering like a mirage on the eastern horizon
is the 'German Village', known as FIBUA. It was built in
the 1990s to replace Imber as a modern training
scenario for fighting in built up areas (hence the
acronym).

The Imber Range perimeter path is a 30-mile
circuit – of the Imber Range! Leaflets are available from
Wiltshire County Council.

It is always a good feeling leaving the metalled road, and once
on the footpath, if the guns are silent up on the Plain, it is a
very tranquil walk through the Ashton Valley, as it is referred to
by Colt Hoare in *Ancient Wiltshire*. Despite its seclusion this
path has the feel of a much travelled route, and the 1773 map
of Wiltshire by Andrews and Dury confirms this. It shows this
and the current Chitterne to Codford road on the opposite side
of the brook as being of equal status – it just depended on
which of the two Codfords was your destination. Ours, for a
while at least, is Codford St Peter.

Near the old windpump at the end of the long grass field lies
a group of barrows that William Cunnington 'opened' between
1801 and 1808. He recorded eleven but I had difficulty now
counting five. The barrow next to the windpump was excavated
on four separate occasions, but yielded very little other than

broken burial urns containing burnt remains and two skeletons. In Upton Lovell William Cunnington uncovered numerous gold artefacts from another Bronze Age barrow situated very near the River Wylye – which he dubbed 'The Golden Barrow'. I wonder whether he believed he might also find gold here next to Chitterne Brook.

5 Just before the next belt of trees (ST 974 421), turn right up the steep field-edge bridleway, and follow a succession of metal bridleway gates for 1.2km.

Different types of barrow, as envisaged by Cunnington and Colt Hoare, and published in 1812. Since their time the typology has developed and some names have changed.

The bridleway that now returns in a westerly direction is an intriguing one. When I used to look after the rights of way in this area I was once told that it was used to carry clay for the making of tobacco pipes in the 17th and 18th centuries. The definitive statement which accompanies the definitive map refers to it as the 'Stardway' or 'Stordway' and reveals that it runs from Heytesbury to Bulford. In the 17th century John Aubrey, the Wiltshire antiquarian, wrote 'Tobacco-pipe-clay excellent, or the best in England, at Chittern, of which the Gauntlet pipes at Amesbury are made . . . They are the best tobacco pipes in England'. Clay Pit Hill is shown on the Ordnance Survey map just inside the Chitterne Parish boundary further east along this route, at ST 995 424. I also checked the colour-coded geological map of the area and the clay pit stands out like a lone purple island of Reading Bed clay in a green sea of Upper Chalk.

Back up on the higher ground and across to the right is the best view so far of an Iron Age field system, which reminds us just how extensively prehistoric cultivation covered this area. A little way ahead (at point 6) there has been a recent authorised diversion of the public rights of way network. The alteration may not appear yet on your Ordnance Survey map, but the new route is clearly marked with signposts.

6 **At the top of the spur turn left for 50 metres, then right, and continue west on the newly diverted path for 900m to a T junction of tracks (ST 954 423), 100m beyond Upton Great Barrow.**

In 1801 William Cunnington was approached by a labourer who, while digging into Upton Great Barrow, was combining treasure hunting with the more prosaic and destructive task of extracting flints from the barrow for turnpike road maintenance. The labourer had found nothing but bones and ashes, but William Cunnington, at the depth of eleven feet, found 'a shallow bason, cut in the native chalk and containing the burnt bones of one person'. Accompanying this primary interment was a selection of beads that had once formed a necklace. Over half the beads were of Baltic Amber, which is a striking indication that the trade routes across Europe had already become established by the Bronze Age. It seems likely from the evidence and also from a lack of prestigious warrior grave goods that this was an individual female burial. Our course takes us within feet of Upton Great Barrow, and it is a pity that it cannot be viewed more easily. Through a gap in the foliage I counted at least fifty mature beech trees growing out of the giant mound, and the whole barrow and outer ditch seem to be enclosed in a pheasant rearing pen with a large water tank perched on top of it. Although this is a rather bizarre function for such a magnificent barrow at least it has not been ploughed out like the nearby 'Bone Barrow'.

THE 'BONE BARROW', which lies about 500m north-east of Upton Great Barrow, was described by the archaeologist Stuart Piggott as being, 'without precise parallel in Britain'. The articles found have more in common with a Siberian Shaman than a Bronze Age warrior. The sixty or so perforated bone points and boar tusks which formed a necklace or some kind of fringe garment are on display in the Wiltshire Heritage Museum at Devizes, along with an assortment of rubbing and polishing stones and stone axes. The 'Bone Barrow' has recently been re-excavated to try to glean more information from the skeletal remains, and to see if perhaps the individual may have in fact been a metal worker. While carrying out the work there was an opportunity to study William Cunnington's excavation methods of two centuries earlier, and the observation was made about the care he had taken to place the larger bones to one side for re-burial. The use of aerial photography and geophysical survey to locate the now ploughed-out barrow, and the planned radiocarbon dating and chemical analysis of the skeletal samples, all serve to illustrate the range of archaeological methods that can be utilised today.

7 Turn left and follow the track straight downhill for 1.3km to meet the A36 road. Cross it with great care and continue towards Upton Lovell. Bear right at the first road junction, then follow the road round to the right near an old horse chestnut tree, continue north-west past (or into!) the *Prince Leopold* pub on the left. Keep straight ahead to the end of this road, then through a metal bridlegate and along the field edge path towards Knook village.

As our route descends into the Wylye Valley, Great Ridge Wood monopolises the horizon, offering fabulous walks and opportunities for solitude and exploration in all seasons of the year (see walk 5, Journey to the Interior, below pages 35-40).

From the middle of the fifteenth century cloth production became an established trade in the Wylye Valley villages, and Upton Lovell, along with Heytesbury and Knook, were all once larger communities and very dependent on the woollen industry. Gradually south Wiltshire was eclipsed by the expanding towns further west, although by the mid-1800s Yorkshire had taken over as the nucleus of the textile industry in England.

In the small church at Knook there are hints as to its Saxon origins, and it seems likely that the incoming Saxons established a settlement here, so finally marking the departure from lofty habitations on the arid upper chalk in favour of the river valley.

8 Outside Knook church (ST 938 418) cross the road and keep ahead on a footpath. After 300m fork right, keeping on the northern side of the River Wylye, and after a further 500m along this footpath you arrive at the old A36 once more. Turn left for Heytesbury.

With our circuit completed we head back into Heytesbury and on the left, set back from the old A36, is William Cunnington's house, now called 'The Old Estate House'. I wonder whether there are any of his prehistoric or geological artefacts remaining in an odd corner of the garden? While walking back through the village I encountered a lady who told me that she had lived in the village all her life. I asked if she had heard of William Cunnington, the great Wiltshire archaeologist. 'William who?' she replied.

William Cunnington is buried in Heytesbury churchyard, and there is a plaque inside the Church which gives a warm account of, 'this persevering antiquary'. Anyone carrying out research into south Wiltshire's prehistory today will undoubtedly be walking in William Cunnington's footsteps.

Further Reading

Cunnington, Robert, 1975, *From Antiquary to Archaeolgist* (Shire)
Hoare, Sir Richard Colt, 1812, *Ancient history of south Wiltshire* (reprinted 1975 by EP Publishing)
McOmish, David *et al*, 2002, *The Field Archaeology of the Salisbury Plain Training Area* (English Heritage)
Marsden, Barry, 1994, *The Early Barrow Diggers* (Tempus)

4 A Downland Odyssey
Bishopstrow and Scratchbury Hill

(5 miles / 8 km)

by Nigel Vile   (OS Explorer 143)

A relatively long and energetic walk across some fine downland to the east of Warminster, where on Scratchbury Hill our steps pass one of the finest hillforts in the area. The views from these lofty heights are far ranging, particularly eastwards across the forbidden military training grounds of Salisbury Plain. Before reaching the high downland, the walk follows flat fieldpaths and lanes in the Wylye Valley near the villages of Bishopstrow and Norton Bavant. Unfortunately, there are no refreshment facilities along the way, although the close-cropped grassland around Scratchbury Hill provides many perfect locations for pausing to enjoy a packed lunch. Although not on the walk itself, it is possible to take a short detour to visit another fine hillfort on Battlesbury Hill.

1 To reach the start from Warminster town-centre take the B3414 for 1 mile south-east, then follow an unclassified road signposted to Sutton Veny. Almost immediately, this road passes through Bishopstrow, where a cul-de-sac lane leads down to the church. Park on the roadside just outside the churchyard (ST 895 438).

Follow the footpath to the right of the church, around the churchyard wall and, where the wall ends, continue to a handgate in the corner of the field and a junction. Bear right along an enclosed grassy path to a metal kissing gate before continuing to the next junction (ST 897 437). Turn left, and follow Watery Lane up to the B3414. Just before the main road, turn right and head across a horse paddock to a bungalow, crossing a series of stiles along the way (SU 901 438).

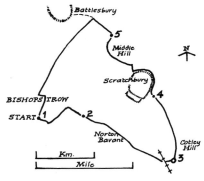

One of the stained glass windows in St Aldhelm's Church depicts the legendary origins of Bishopstrow – the Bishop's Tree. The church stands near the spot where St Aldhelm once preached, prior to conducting a number of baptisms in the River Wylye. The legend relates how St Aldhelm plunged his staff into the ground, and how it took root before developing into an ash tree. The two other stained glass windows in the church depict members of the local landed gentry. A window of 1892 is dedicated to Vere de Lane Temple, whose ancestral home is Bishopstrow House, now a fine country hotel, while a window of 1900 is dedicated to Arthur Melville Southey of Eastleigh Court, whose 19th-century home and parkland lie to the west of the village. Bishopstrow itself is little more than a single village street lined on both sides by rows of small cottages. A number of these dwellings were thatched until the 1930s, when sadly destroyed by fire. My favourite building in the village, however, remains the green and white cricket pavilion, constructed of that most flexible of building materials – corrugated iron! The setting of pavilion and cricket square, overshadowed by the

The Cricket Pavilion, Bishopstrow

spire of St Aldhelm's Church, provides a perfect cameo of traditional English life.

2 Enter the field to the left of the bungalow, and follow the right-hand field boundary past a barn and on to a gap in the far right corner. Bear right through this gap, then left along a grassy track to a minor crossroads in 100m on the fringes of Norton Bavant (ST 906 436). Follow the lane ahead for 400m to the next crossroads, keep straight ahead and, in 200m, where this lane bears right, keep ahead along a cul-de-sac lane to a stile by the Old Bakery. Follow the right edge of the next field to a gap, before heading diagonally across the next field to a railway bridge in its far left-hand corner (ST 916 429).

All Saints Church in Norton Bavant is largely a 19th-century rebuilding, although the tower dates back to the 14th century, with the entrance arch to the Benett Chapel dating from the 13th century. This entrance arch, clearly removed from its original location, appears to have been placed most unceremoniously at ground level to the rear of the church. The Benetts are commemorated within All Saints Church by brasses of two husbands – John and Thomas Benett – and their wives, one with two groups of children. As with so many English churches, All Saints is normally locked for security reasons, although a notice in the porch gives details of access arrangements. Alongside the church stands Norton Bavant House, with its seven bays, cross-windows and hipped roof creating a most handsome residence. Above the doorway is a fine shell-hood on carved brackets, dating back to the time of Queen Anne. The house itself is even older, with a contract of 1641 in existence.

3 By this bridge, follow the path that climbs up to the right to join the B3095. Turn left, and follow the road over the railway and up to a roundabout. Cross the B3414 exit from this roundabout, before following the signposted bridleway opposite that climbs the hillside. This is in fact the course of an inclined plane that ran downhill from hilltop quarries. At the top of the climb, cross the level hilltop enclosure, passing various tumuli, to a stile in the end field boundary. Cross to the far right corner of the next field and a stile below the ramparts surrounding Scratchbury Hill (ST 914 442).

A short detour along one of the minor roads that leaves the A36 roundabout will bring you into Heytesbury – indeed, until late

All Saints Church, Norton Bavant

1986, when the local bypass was opened, the main trunk road ran through the heart of the village. This was an ancient borough, which to this day exudes a great sense of history. Heytesbury was Hungerford territory, the famous Walter Hungerford becoming Treasurer of England back in 1428. As well as founding and endowing a chapel at Salisbury Cathedral, Walter Hungerford established Heytesbury's almshouses, officially known as the 'Hospital of St John'. Today's almshouses are a rebuilding, a serious fire in 1770 destroying the original building. The interested visitor will also discover a lock-up or 'blind house' alongside the almshouses, as well as the Jacobean Parsonage Farm behind the church. St Peter and St Paul's itself is an impressive building, cruciform in layout with a central tower.

There is also an element of industrial history in this corner of the walk. The bridleway that climbs on to Cotley Hill really does appear to be too flat and symmetrical to be a natural

HILLFORTS Iron Age hillforts are a common feature of the chalk uplands of Wiltshire. Perhaps the best description of a hillfort is an enclosure, apparently fortified, for use as a cattle compound or settlement varying from several dwellings to something the size of a small town. The simplest hillforts consisted of a palisade or stockade of heavy timbers set in a trench interlaced with wattles and thorny material. The material excavated from the ditch was used to build up the rampart mound. This construction of single earthwork and ditch was known as 'univallate'. Advances in weaponry necessitated improvements in defences, including the development of two or more closely set banks and ditches, known as 'multivallate'. The hillfort's strength was in using the lie of the land to make it very difficult to attack, and also to make the enclosed area safe by erecting these various banks and ditches. The passage of time has silted up the defensive trenches; grasses, bushes and trees have in some cases overgrown the site. Despite this, there are throughout Britain more than 2,500 embanked and ditched enclosures, whose contour-hugging ramparts offer a wide sweep of far-reaching views.

feature. A map of 1773 is labelled with 'a channel cut in the side of the hill for the easy conveying of stone from the quarries'. This was in fact an inclined plane, which carried chalk and flint from the hilltop down to what was then a coach road. On reaching the hilltop, the pitted and pock-marked ground, similar to the gruffy ground where lead was worked on Mendip, is the site of the old stone quarries.

4 Follow the ramparts to the right. In 200m, at the north-eastern corner of the hillfort, bear left and follow the lower rampart around the northern edge of the hillfort. In 200m cross a stile in the fence on the right and continue downhill in the next field to another stile and a lane. Turn left and, at a junction in 20m (ST 910 447), enter a field and climb Middle Hill to reach the top left corner of the field by a small copse. Bear left into the next field, and follow the fence on the left. In 250m, where this fence ends, continue walking ahead across the hillside before dropping downhill to join a military road (ST 907 453).

The hillfort atop Scratchbury Hill dates from late prehistory. The double-banked fort with a ditch between enclosed a huge area of some 37 acres. Within the hillfort site lies evidence of an earlier Iron Age enclosure as well as five Bronze Age round barrows. The hillfort itself lies on a spur overlooking the Wylye Valley, and the views are never less than impressive. Below, beyond the Warminster Road, lies the River Wylye, with Cold Kitchen Hill prominent in the distance. To the north lies the isolated hillock of Cley Hill, while eastward lies the military training grounds of Salisbury Plain.

Beyond Scratchbury Hill lies Middle Hill, which unusually for these downlands was never the site of a hillfort or some other such occupancy. Its chief archaeological features are quite simply a fine collection of strip lynchets on its eastern slopes and a solitary hilltop barrow. The open chalk downland hereabouts is home to a rich variety of flora. In Spring and early summer, cowslips, harebells, trefoil and common milkwort abound, while it should be possible to discover the occasional wild orchid.

Barrow on Middle Hill

5 Turn right and, in 20m, climb some steps on the left and follow the right edge of the field ahead up to its top right corner and a junction of paths (ST 904 455). The path ahead leads on to Battlesbury Hill – an almost obligatory detour. For the main walk, turn left and follow a grassy ride down to the MoD road, with Battlesbury Hill rising away on the right-hand side. Cross this concrete road, and follow the track opposite over the railway and on down to the B3414 (ST 895442). Turn left along to a rank of cottages. Opposite the end cottage – Old Stones – cross the road and follow the footpath opposite signposted to Bishopstrow Church. Follow this path across the Wylye and down to a lane, before continuing ahead back to the church.

SALISBURY PLAIN AND THE IMBER RANGES The landscape to the east of this walk, containing the village of Imber, was closed to the public in 1943, and has been used by the Army for live firing ever since. Most of Imber's residents accepted their eviction fatalistically. 'I lived to die here,' said one elderly lady of 88, 'but must is with the King'. Many were consoled by the fact that their removal would be only temporary, but such hopes were short-lived as time reduced the numbers of original Imber inhabitants. There were regular protests and 'invasions' of the now forbidden territory, these increasing in number until the War Office obtained injunctions against the marchers in 1961. That summer, a public inquiry chaired by Sir Harold Emmerson and Alan Lubbock was held in Trowbridge. Evidence was heard from all parties, and the Crown finally recommended the complete closure of the area and all of its ancient rights of way. Access to the area is still permitted, however, by the MoD during most public holidays, with access being along the four metalled roads that run from Warminster, Heytesbury, Gore Cross and Bratton. Somewhat ironically, although military activity has scarred the landscape, the army's occupancy of the Plain has prevented any real human development. A rich flora and fauna has developed on what is one of the true wilderness areas in Southern Britain.

Battlesbury Hill is topped out with a magnificent Iron Age hillfort. Active in approximately 50 BC, Battlesbury was in all probability a permanent settlement, judging by the artifacts discovered in the vicinity. These ancient remains included pottery fragments, iron keys and saws, as well as part of a chariot wheel. Rotary quern stones would also suggest that corn was grown in the area. This multivallate fort extended around a 25-acre enclosure, with entrances protected to the north-west and east by smaller outworks. Somewhat ironically, the ancient defensive fortification overlooks a significant part of Britain's current defences at nearby Battlesbury Barracks in Warminster.

Further Reading

Pevsner, Nikolaus ,1963, *The Buildings of England: Wiltshire* (Penguin).
Woodruffe, Brian, 1982, *Wiltshire villages* (Hale)

5 Journey to the Interior

Sherrington and Great Ridge (7 miles/ 11 km)

by Roger Jones   (OS Explorer 143)

A lengthy but gentle walk with a gradual ascent from the 85 metre contour in the village to 214 metres at Great Ridge (that's over 400 feet in old money!). On leaving the charming environs of Sherrington, we are soon gazing towards the thickly wooded heights of Great Ridge. A steady climb takes us to this tree-filled landscape where the birds (and deer if you are lucky) are our only company. If you wish to get away from it all and are seeking complete peace and quiet then this is the walk for you.

Wiltshire's chalk downland is scored by many valleys, for example the wide Vale of Pewsey, which separates the Marlborough Downs and Salisbury Plain, and those valleys

Cottage across the Sherrington watercress beds

(including this, the Wylye) which carry streams towards Salibury to join the Avon flowing from Pewsey Vale. The Wylye Valley also provides a route for the A36 trunk road and the railway line from Salisbury to the towns of West Wiltshire and beyond. The downland above the village provides extensive pasture for cattle, though few sheep are to be seen today. The woods along Great Ridge are also an important natural resource where much logging takes place. Sherrington is a most attractive village, its cottages scattered about the former watercress beds, while its interesting old church stands beside the fast-flowing Wylye.

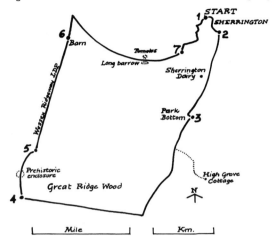

1 The walk begins at Sherrington church (ST 960 392), which is approached by narrow lanes. Parking near the church without causing annoyance is therefore difficult, and you should be prepared to find a suitable place to stop on the edge of the village and walk to the church. We shall postpone an exploration of Sherrington until our walk is complete. With your back to the church bear left and follow the lane for 300m until you reach the minor road which traverses the south side of the Wylye Valley.

Like many of Wiltshire's valleys, settlements grew up along the spring line, where water percolating down through the porous chalk meets the impervious Gault clay. Sherrington is one such village, the spring water here filling wide ponds in which the cultivation of watercress was carried out on quite a large scale, with the chalk escarpment rising up directly south of the village like a protective arm. Before crossing the road note the green sunken lane between the tarmac to your right. This is not a right of way but leads down to one such spring, at the level where chalk meets clay, which then flows into the watercress beds.

2 Cross the road bearing a little to the left and take the signposted bridleway which heads uphill. This track

between boundary hedges, sunken with age, very soon reaches a junction of ways. Cross over and continue straight ahead, rising gradually.

Soon revealed is a panorama of sweeping downland, huge arable fields and woodland, occasional copses giving way to the dense tree cover on Great Ridge. Once we pass the low buildings of Sherrington Dairy on the right there are really no signs of buildings to be seen.

3 The track ends at a gate where we bear left to reach a metalled lane (ST 958 375). This leads to a dwelling about half a mile further on given on the Explorer map as 'High Grove Cottage'. Turn right at the lane and head on until it swings to the left to reach High Grove Cottage. Do not follow it, but continue in the same direction as previously up a rough track signposted 'Road used as a Public Path'. All the time we are climbing gradually, there is a shoulder of woodland on the right and denser beech woodland approaching to our left. The track begins to level out as we reach a gate on our right. Proceed through this gate and enjoy a wide green track for more than a mile until you reach a junction of ways (ST 931 361).

The woodland is delightfully varied up here: alternate plantations of larch and pine to your left, but spaced sufficiently far apart to allow much green undergrowth, while to the right there flourishes a genuine wildwood – gnarled oaks smothered with ivy. You will pass lookouts at intervals beside the track – you can climb one of these to survey the scene from a height of about 10 feet; you may be rewarded with the sight of deer. The nearest I came to doing so one March day was stumbling over a well gnawed leg. The tree cover thins out as you approach the junction of tracks, particularly to the right. The ground appears to be rather boggy hereabouts – an indication of a deposit of clay-with-flints forming an impervious layer above the chalk bedrock. There is a noticeboard here displaying a map of the area.

4 At the junction of ways turn right, ignore the path on the right, but, just before reaching a surfaced track at the T-junction ahead, look out for the remains of a prehistoric enclosure. Its earthworks are in the form of two curving arms either side of your path. The section on the right is easier to trace: you can make out the rampart (on the inside of the curve) and the ditch (on the outside).

Cross the road at the T-junction and continue directly ahead, walking between pairs of newly planted, fenced trees which will eventually form an avenue here. The right of way bears a little to the right until another junction of ways is reached.

The Explorer map indicates woodland to the left as 'Corton Wood' and 'Picket Grove', but the bulk of the trees here appear to have been felled. Indeed, there is much evidence of logging activity in the vicinity.

We are now about to follow the Wessex Ridgeway Long Distance Path. Wiltshire is criss-crossed by a number of such designated pedestrian routes; the Wessex Ridgeway begins in Marlborough and ends in Lyme Regis, a total distance of 219km (136 miles).

5 **Bear left (at ST 932 369) beside the forest on your right. From this point the straight path ahead is pretty much level.**

First the prospect to the left opens up: you can see up the Wylye valley towards Warminster. Arn Hill above the town and Battlesbury Hill before it look like a brace of ships cruising in from the east, an advance guard of Salisbury Plain. Further west may be seen the distinctive outline of Cley Hill, and further west again the Mohican hairstyle appearance of Long Knoll, near the Somerset border, both features being outliers of chalk. A little further along, the view east, looking down the Wylye Valley, opens out, though there are few distinctive features in that direction.

6 **A mile along the Wessex Ridgeway (at ST 938 388) we pass a barn beside the track and an elevated water tank. Just behind this tank lurks a triangulation pillar marking the high point of 187 metres. From here a pleasanter alternative is the enclosed path which runs parallel to the farm track. At the junction ahead (ST 939 392) you change direction by turning sharp right along a metalled lane. You may meet an occasional vehicle here but the overwhelming calm means you will be well aware of any approaching motors. Follow the metalled road beside some woodland on the left and barns on the right.**

Look out for an overgrown long barrow beside the road on the right and a distinctive round barrow ('tumulus' on the Explorer map) in the field to the left. The parish boundary between

Sherrington and Boyton, first recorded as an estate boundary in the 10th century, uses both barrows as landmarks, and one is referred to in a document of 968 as 'Maiden Barrow'.

Looking across the Wylye valley to Codford from Maiden Barrow

7 **About 500m beyond these features (at ST 956 386) you forsake the road and bear left along a track above the escarpment, below which lies Sherrington. As you descend look out for a wooden step stile on the left. Pause here awhile to savour the view. Beyond the village, across the railway track and the A36 lie the Codfords; the church towers at Codford St Peter and Codford St Mary may both be picked out. Cross the stile and head down the field to the stile below. You now descend by the sunken footpath, no doubt worn into the chalk by countless generations of local bipeds. It is this sort of footpath archaeology which, for me, imbues old rights of way with a special magic. Bear to the right and leave the field by the stile in the bottom right hand corner to reach the road (ST 959 389). Cross this road and go through the gate to enter the field opposite. Cross this field but bear right to reach a stile above the old watercress ponds. Head across the footbridge made of old railway sleepers until you reach the lane opposite. Bear right.**

The village dwellings are all pleasing to the eye – there is much well maintained thatch, and walls built of chalk rock (also known by the delightful term 'clunch') – sometimes with flint infill. You pass the nostalgically named Cress Cottage, and as you bear right towards the church, note the Bible texts attached high up on the gable of the cottage at the corner – also the parish notice board given to mark the Coronation in 1953 (the bus shelter up on the road was erected to mark the Silver Jubilee in 1977).

Now for Sherrington's chief delight: its medieval church rebuilt (unusually) in the early-17th century. It is superbly sited on a little knoll beside the clear waters of the Wylye and the lane which encircles the village. Behind it, tree-covered and inaccessible, are the remains of a small motte and bailey castle. The church is a small building – just a nave, chancel, belfry and porch. One side of the porch is filled with contemporary memorial tablets and the other with news of services and other events linked to the church, evidently still very much a centre of life in this community.

Inside the church you notice first its many windows, which render it bright and airy, even though it is a comparatively small structure. The many wall texts date from earlier centuries, presumably whitewashed over in Puritan times, but restored in 1939. Most interesting of all is the church's unusual dedication: to Saints Cosmas and Damian. These we are told were twin Arabian martyrs and doctors. Their story is graphically told, in words and pictures, in a frame hanging on the wall. I won't give it away here, suffice it to say that it features an account of spare-part surgery in the fourth century. The children will love the gruesome details.

This wonderful building, full of old stone and wood and superbly situated beside the River Wylye, makes a fitting finale to this memorable journey to the interior of Wiltshire.

Further Reading

Victoria History of Wiltshire, 1995, vol. 15, pp. 234-42
Willoughby, Rosamund, 1998, *Sherrington: a Wiltshire village* (privately published)

6 The Stonehenge Walk

(4.8 miles/ 7.7km)

by Julian Richards   (OS Explorer 130)

It's very easy to visit Stonehenge, park the car, walk under the road and round the stones and not realize what a stupendous prehistoric landscape it sits in. But if you have the inclination, some of the best Neolithic and Bronze Age monuments in southern England are there to be explored. This walk not only takes in some wonderful archaeological sites but you can also feel that you are walking in the footsteps of some of the great pioneering antiquarians and archaeologists of the past two centuries.

1 It's quite simple. Just take the gate at the lower end of the car park and turn right on to the rough track that heads north towards Larkhill. Already you will see great burial mounds silhouetted against the skyline in the field on your left. These are what you are heading for, but look out for the stile in the fence on your left. Cross it and head for the barrows (SU 120 428), part of what is known as the 'Cursus Group' (for reasons that will become apparent very shortly).

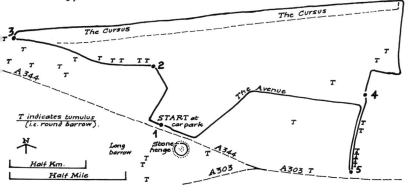

The bigger mounds that you are now approaching are fine examples of bell barrows, distinguished from the more common bowl barrows by having a flat area (or 'berm') separating the mound from the surrounding ditch, the quarry for the mound material. This produces a profile for which the term bell is very apt. These are just part of a group of barrows that lies along the chalk ridge, parallel to the Stonehenge Cursus (next on the itinerary) and designed to be highly visible. Today their grassy contours blend into the surrounding landscape, but when they were first built they would have stood out as mounds of gleaming white chalk, proclaiming the wealth and importance of the individuals buried within them. Like almost all the barrows in this area these have been excavated and the tell tale signs of exploration can be seen in the hollowed summits of the mounds.

The Cursus Barrow

The wealthy landowner Sir Richard Colt Hoare and his archaeological companion William Cunnington were the diggers, and the fruits of their labours can be seen in the museum at Devizes, fine pottery, bronze weapons and personal ornaments and the occasional fabulous piece of goldwork. These burials are of the rich and powerful of the early Bronze Age, dating back to around 2000 - 1800BC, the time that Stonehenge itself was nearing completion.

2 **Follow the line of the barrows and head off towards the gap in the woods that lie ahead (SU 112 429). This involves veering off slightly to your right. As you approach the gap look out for a low bank and ditch heading in the same direction.**

This is the northern side of the Stonehenge Cursus. This enigmatic monument was first recorded by the great 18th-century antiquarian William Stukeley, who, in the unploughed downland turf observing an enclosure defined by a ditch and bank, about 100m wide and over 2.5km long. You are now heading for the western end of this strange monument, which Stukely christened the 'Cursus' as he believed it to be Roman in date and a 'hippodrome' or race track (presumably for chariot racing). If you walk through the clearing in the wood, deliberately created to show the width of the Cursus, you will come to a single small bronze age barrow and beyond this a reconstructed section of the terminal bank and ditch. If you turn and look back then you can see the whole length of the Cursus which stretches as far as the belt of trees on the near horizon.

But what is it? This is something to ponder as you walk its full length. Are you following in the footsteps of Neolithic processions, making a solemn pilgrimage along a sacred avenue to carry out ceremonies at the ends of the enclosure? Here the banks and ditches were originally much larger, giving a 'grandstand' like appearance. The answer is that we really don't know, a lot of effort has clearly gone into building what to many is seen as a processional way, but the rituals that may have been carried out within it have left no trace in the archaeological record.

Towards King Barrow Ridge

3 If the idea of walking further is just too much then you can return to the car park from here or you can walk half the Cursus and then take the gravel track back to the car park. But, if you want more, then do the full length of the Cursus and then, after pausing to look back along it from the eastern end (SU 137 432), take the track to the right that runs alongside the wood.

You are now on the King Barrow Ridge heading towards some of the biggest and finest barrows in the whole Stonehenge landscape. You will first start to catch glimpses of some of them to your right in the woods, scattered mounds, some in small clearings surrounded by trees, others isolated in grassy fields.

4 **These are the Old King Barrows but, after taking a dog leg in the track, first a right, then a left, you will pass an ancient yew wood in which there are yet more mounds and head towards the group known as the New King Barrows (SU 134 423).**

It is, however, worth pausing in the gap just after the yew wood and looking back to Stonehenge. This is one of the best long views of the stones, giving a true appreciation of their setting in its wider landscape, a natural amphitheatre rimmed with groups of barrows. Sometimes, even the modern intrusions of roads and car parks seem to melt away.

This is also the spot, in the open space that you are now about to cross, where the Avenue runs across the ridge before sweeping downhill and turning towards Stonehenge. The Avenue is a formal approach to Stonehenge's main north-east facing entrance and here, like the Cursus, a processional way has been defined by low banks and ditches. It originally curved off to the left of the track, under the A303 and down to where it joins the River Avon at West Amesbury, but centuries of ploughing have leveled these ditches and banks. You will see the only short surviving section on your way back to Stonehenge.

But first, the New King Barrows. Until 1987 it was almost impossible to appreciate the scale of these barrows as they lay in an ancient tangled beech wood, covered in trees and fallen

King Barrows

branches. The great storm that took place in that year devastated the wood, allowing the National Trust who had just bought the land to expose the mounds which now lie in grassy clearings, surrounded by the gnarled survivors of the storm. These are the only barrows in the Stonehenge landscape to retain their secrets as, when Colt Hoare and Cunnington were conducting their campaigns of excavation in the early 1800s, the barrows were covered in trees and they could not get permission to dig. Their scale, huge mounds, some of which have been shown by examining holes left by the roots of fallen trees to have been made largely of turf, suggests that they must contain important burials, but precisely what, we may never know.

5 **If you have seen all of the New King Barrows then you should be almost at the A303. Do not try to cross the road! Retrace your steps along the track until you reach the stile in the left hand fence. At first there is nothing to guide you so head off across the grass until, as you come over the crest of the ridge you see the line of the avenue in the bottom of the dry valley and its ditches and banks heading off towards Stonehenge. Walk down into the dry valley.**

I am sure that this was the only way to enter Stonehenge in the time that it was in use as a great temple. Maybe the only way was to go down to the river and wade in its cleansing waters before walking the curving line of the Avenue to this point. Pause and turn towards the Stones for the final short walk into the sacred circles. Imagine being here at the time of the Summer or Winter solstice, Stonehenge wasn't built as an ancient monument but as a living temple. Imagine the people that would gather here, perhaps from all over southern England, perhaps from beyond. Imagine the ceremonies.

This is a good place to imagine, but the reality is now a short walk back to the Stonehenge car park and the completion of what is still one of my favourite Wiltshire walks.

Further Reading

Chippindale, Christopher, 1983, *Stonehenge complete* (Thames & Hudson)

Richards, Julian, 1991, *English Heritage book of Stonehenge* (English Heritage)

Souden, David, 1997, *Stonehenge: mysteries of the stones and landscape* (Collins & Brown)

. . . and many others!

7 Valley of the Enigma

Great Durnford, Wilsford and Upper Woodford (7.5 miles, 12 km)

by John Chandler   (OS Explorer 130)

The peaceful scenery and beauty of the Woodford Valley (as the stretch of the Avon from Amesbury to Salisbury is known) are themselves ample justification for including this walk. But since 1987, when The Enigma of Arrival *was published, the countryside around Wilsford has become familiar to millions of readers worldwide as the setting for V S Naipaul's masterpiece. For anyone who has read the book and absorbed its landscape, this walk will provide an afternoon of recognition; for anyone who has not, it will offer a gentle but irresistible introduction to an outstanding work of literature. The walk features two villages, Great Durnford and Wilsford, on opposite sides of the valley, together with several smaller settlements, and riverside, woodland and downland scenery. Opportunities for extending and curtailing it are given, and the itinerary includes two excellent pubs.*

1 **Park considerately in the village street of Great Durnford, near the *Black Horse* pub (SU 135 379). Walk northwards along the village street, noting (and if you wish, visiting) St Andrew's parish church set back on the left, and approached by a track alongside a cob wall. Just beyond the church turning the street becomes a cul de sac, and you should follow the minor road round to the right.**

A peaceful place of handsome farmhouses and cottages along its lane, Great Durnford polarised in the middle ages around its south end (the area of the pub and the mill) and its north end (the church, Church Farm and later the manor house). Each half farmed and managed its land separately. The exquisite church,

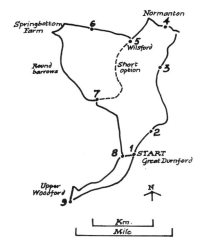

which has always served most of the eastern side of the Woodford valley, retains a feast of Norman work, including fine sculpture, as well as good later woodwork and fittings. James Harris, a writer around whom cultured society in Georgian Salisbury pivoted, lived in a since-demolished house near the church. His namesake son, a diplomat who was created the first earl of Malmesbury, bought the north end manor in 1791 and built the elegant brick manor house within its landscaped park, thereby closing off the northern end of the village street.

2 The lane climbs the hill in a tree-lined Greensand cutting and then descends again. This is known as Diamond Bottom. Immediately beyond a yellow brick house on the left take the bridleway left into the woods (SU 141 386). When the track levels out there are long views on the

View across the valley to Wilsford church and manor house

right across Salisbury Plain to Sidbury. As soon as the track leaves the wood take the smaller path to the right, continue through a metal gate and along the top edge of the field to the right.

The view across the valley which now opens in front of you takes in Wilsford church (to the right) and Wilsford Manor (to the left), both shrouded in trees. In between, and within the grounds of the manor house, stands the cottage (actually a bungalow) around which *The Enigma of Arrival* is set. The tree-lined track climbing the hillside behind the valley buildings leads to Springbottom, and will later on be part of this walk.

3 **At a cross-roads of tracks continue straight across a second field to another metal gate, then follow the fenceline at the foot of the scarp, along a path close to the river. Cross by the second footbridge you come to (SU 142 401), which goes over a small stream, and follow the path to the footbridge across the main river, its course here narrowed and controlled by hatches. Cross also the small brick bridge beyond.**

Footbridge across the Avon, by Normanton House

Normanton House, originally built as a farmhouse in the 18th century, together with a few cottages nearby, are all that remain as successors to the medieval hamlet of Normanton, which in the middle ages had its own chapel of ease. Settlement shrinkage, and occasionally complete desertion, have occurred along the whole length of the south Wiltshire river valleys, as some villages have prospered and others declined. Like its neighbours, Normanton had its share of meadowland by the river, arable fields on the hillside behind the present house, and rough downland beyond. Normanton Down extends in a narrow strip for some 3km until it reaches and just crosses the present A303 main road near Stonehenge.

4 **Aim for the cob wall at the far end of the paddock, veer left slightly, and join the driveway to Normanton House, heading for the gateposts and iron gates which lead you out into the minor (but busy – take care!) valley road (SU 137 402). Turn left (southwards) and follow the lane for some 400m until you see the sign for Springbottom Farm on the right. Shortly you will take this turning, but first continue another 100m along the valley road to visit Wilsford Church.**

Although it has a simple Norman tower, Wilsford church is largely a dull effort by the Victorian architect T H Wyatt. But it is enlivened by an unrivalled collection of monuments, including (inside) a slate memorial by Eric Gill, and (outside) a headstone (to Pamela Grey) by Rex Whistler. Wilsford Manor, in 17th-century style, was in fact built in 1904-6 to designs by the Arts and Crafts architect Detmar Blow. His client, Edward Tennant, Lord Glenconner, was heir to a fortune derived from chemicals, and the house descended to the eccentric and reclusive dilettante, Stephen Tennant. He was Naipaul's landlord in *The Enigma of Arrival*, and is memorably described in the novel's third section; he died in 1987, the year of the book's publication, and his house and its contents were sold.

5 **You can shorten the walk by continuing down the valley road to Lake, then turning right along the tarmac road for some 600m until you reach a crossroads of tracks just beyond the last house. This is point 7 below. The longer and more rewarding route takes you back to the Springbottom Farm turning (SU 135 399), up the tarmac track to farm buildings and a covered reservoir, then continuing down the track towards Springbottom Farm. As you descend you should look across to the right for views across the Stonehenge landscape.**

Springbottom is the setting for 'Jack's Garden', the first section of Naipaul's book, and this track, with its viewpoint to Stonehenge, is described very early on. The high hills seen from here are Beacon Hill beyond Amesbury (on the right), Sidbury beyond Tidworth (further left), and then the eye scans straight over the central compartment of Salisbury Plain. In the middle ground the traffic along the A303 is easy to spot, but Stonehenge less so (it gradually rises to the horizon as you

V S NAIPAUL was born in Trinidad in 1932 of Indian ancestry, and came to England in 1950 to study at Oxford University. His outstanding writing career, pursued for five decades in England and many countries of the third world, began in 1954. His achievement was acknowledged in 2001 by the award of the Nobel Prize in Literature. In his fiction, essays and travel writing he has become the chronicler of colonial demise and its aftermath. *The Enigma of Arrival* (1987), which was singled out for particular praise in the Nobel citation, is a novel founded on the author's personal journey of observation and discovery. The object of attention is rural Wiltshire around his home in the Woodford valley – a peopled landscape of orderly cycles, gradual change and occasional drama. It is a small canvas, slowly but painstakingly layered to portray a whole world – of nature, society and philosophy – in microcosm. For local people, who are familiar with the real underlying places, and some of whom may even underlie Naipaul's characters, *The Enigma of Arrival* will always hold a very special significance. It is a book to delight, just as the Woodford Valley is a landscape to delight.

descend, and then disappears from view). In places the downland landscape is darkened by blocks of woodland, including (from right to left) Normanton Gorse, Fargo Plantation and the Longbarrow crossroads.

The remote settlement at Springbottom typifies the agricultural change that occurred on the south Wiltshire chalkland manors during the 19th century. The old medieval pattern of open fields on the hillslopes farmed from the riverside settlements below gave way to enclosed, parcelled-up territories, often with new farm complexes built in their midst. At Springbottom only a well house is marked near here on maps until the 1820s, but by 1846 the agriculture of almost the whole of Wilsford was controlled by the tenant farmer living at 'Down Farm', as Springbottom was known when it was first established.

6 Descend to Springbottom and follow the tarmac road around to the left of the buildings. After the furthest house and before the last farm buildings turn sharp left to pick up a byway, which runs as a broad green swathe between fenced horse enclosures on the left and woodland on the right. Follow this byway for more than 1km as it slowly bends to the left and gently descends in a coombe. Notice round barrows on the right and a derelict building amid trees. Then, soon after passing under power lines, you meet a crossroad of tracks, with woodland to your left (SU 129 389).

Settlement movement and shrinkage (as at Normanton) has occurred at Lake, too, but here it is more obvious, because the tell-tale earthworks of vanished buildings, gardens and paddocks have survived as 'humps and bumps' along the lower slopes of the parkland in front of you. Lake House, on the hill to the right, presides over this parkland. It is a fine Elizabethan house, rebuilt by Detmar Blow in 1898 and then rebuilt again after a devastating fire in 1912. It has had a number of interesting owners, including antiquaries and collectors, a brewer who invented equipment for measuring colours, and more recently a celebrated rock musician.

7 Take the footpath southwards (which is a right turn if you have come from Springbottom, a left turn if you have shortened the walk and come from Lake). Enter the wood and take the path to the left, which shortly fringes the wood (on its right) with parkland (and fine distant views) to its left. Notice the large round barrow in the top corner of the park. Climb the stile by a gate and cross the road to the thatched cottage opposite. Take the bridleway which begins immediately in front of it and descends to the right gradually towards the river. You will begin to hear the splashing water of the mill race at Kingfisher (Durnford) Mill.

Kingfisher Mill, Durnford

This is the mill of Great Durnford's South End manor, and is mentioned in a document of 1389 after its owner had fallen into debt. Like many mill sites, however, it is probably much older, and one of the three Saxon mills at Durnford mentioned in Domesday Book is likely to have been here. It worked as a mill until the early 20th century and after falling into disrepair was converted to a house, Kingfisher Mill, after 1960. Its owner and restorer, Aylmer Tryon, published a description of the house, its garden and wildlife, in 1985.

8 **Cross the river hatches and millstream by two bridges (SU 133 379) to go right past the mill and then along its poplar and willow-lined drive. You emerge on to Great Durnford village street close to where you parked. You could end the walk here, by visiting the *Black Horse* perhaps. Or, if you still have the energy you could add another rewarding 3km or so to your walk by turning right and setting off away from the village southwards along the lane. You pass a substantial chalk quarry on your left and a particularly fine bending stretch of the river on your right. Eventually at the T junction turn right and cross the river by Woodford Bridge (SU 124 371), the only road bridge between Stratford sub Castle and Amesbury. The *Bridge Inn*, another excellent Woodford Valley pub, is in front of you.**

The parish of Woodford, which gives this part of the Avon valley its local name, lies exclusively on the west side of the river, the right bank. From Saxon times until the 20th century the manor of Woodford was part of the bishop of Salisbury's estate, and apart from the subordinate manor of Heale, it was always farmed and managed from its three villages, Upper, Middle and Lower Woodford, each a kilometre apart, and all lying along the sinuous valley road. Upper Woodford, to which you have crossed, is the largest of the three and has most of the older houses; it also has the only road bridge across the river (a bridge here is mentioned in 1370). Despite this, it has had neither church, school, vicarage, mill or manor house – they all belong to its rivals.

9 **From the pub walk northwards (right as you face the pub with the river behind you) along the valley road for 200m, to a signed footpath on the right along a gravel drive in front of railings (SU 125 374). The drive becomes a track, which bears left, and you should follow it for about 1km up the valley, as it gradually converges on the river, with water meadows between. You will hear rushing water**

again and find yourself at point 8. From here retrace your steps past the mill and along its drive to Great Durnford village street, where you began.

Further Reading

Drury, Michael, 2000, *Wandering Architects: in Pursuit of an Arts and Crafts ideal* (Shaun Tyas)

Hoare, Philip, 1990, *Serious Pleasures: the life of Stephen Tennant* (Hamilton)

Naipaul, V S, 1987, *The Enigma of Arrival* (Viking/ Penguin)

Tryon, Aylmer, 1985, *Kingfisher Mill* (Collins)

Victoria History of Wiltshire, vols. 6 (for Wilsford, Lake and Woodford) and 15 (for Durnford and Normanton)

8 And All Grovely!

Land of Oak Apple Origins

(5 miles/ 8 km + 1 .5 miles/ 2..5 km)

by Victoria Coombes   (OS Explorer 130)

This circuit starts in Great Wishford, 10 km to the north-west of Salisbury in the heart of the scenic Wylye valley. After touching the banks of the river and exploring one of Wiltshire's prettiest villages, famous for its Oak Apple Day celebrations, it climbs into the shadow of Grovely Woods. Among ancient woodland the walk follows a section of Roman Road along a majestic beech avenue and through varied plantations of conifers and deciduous trees. From the wooded heights there are breathtaking views of the gently curving landscape which stretches across either side of the valley. It is an excellent route for groups as it follows wide tracks which are well-marked. The route through the wood has an easy climb, with no stiles, while the village section includes gentle slopes and crosses three stiles at field edges. There is a pub and a shop in Great Wishford.

There are two variations to this walk. Both begin at the Royal Oak *which has a small car park available to walkers (see box). One uses stages 1 – 3 of the walk to explore the village and covers not much more than two km. This may suit the less energetic who are happy to patronise the pub while awaiting the return of their companions from the longer circuit. The second route starts with the tour of the village and then climbs into Grovely Woods to enjoy views over the valley and the splendour of extensive plantings of mature trees.*

1 The walk begins from The *Royal Oak*, Great Wishford (SU 078 355). Turning back towards the village start by taking the lane signed to Little Langford, Hanging Langford and Wylye. The road drops down a short slope before a left

THE ROYAL OAK Although once known as *The Tap* its name now makes it part of the Oak Apple scene. *The Royal Oak* is currently owned by Nick and Sarah Deschamps who also offer bed and breakfast. It has a small car park which the Deschamps are happy to be used by walkers out of pub opening hours. Their catering specialities are a Sunday Carvery and a £5 Hot Lunch Buffet from Monday to Friday. For those interested in village history there is a copy of a manuscript map dated 1698 on the wall of the restaurant which shows the village as consisting only of a line of houses along South and West Street.

hand bend. Turn right here, where the footpath is signed off to the right and a stile beside a gate leads into a riverside field, where sheep are often grazing (SU 077 357).

A footbridge over the river Wylye, famed for its trout fishing, provides a good point to linger, but is not part of this route. Here herons may be standing motionless as they stare into the clear water, or grey wagtails seen twitching their tails as they bob at the river's edge.

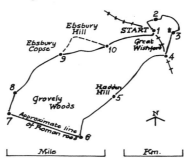

2 The path leaves the river to meet the farm track at a high stile. Cross on to the track and walk a few metres northwards to the left before entering the field on the right through a wooden gate. Here the route runs beside the fence, rather than the river, and follows a right hand curve to meet up with the road just west of Stoford bridge. Once this footpath was the driveway to Wishford Manor and is known locally as Maiden's Walk. There is another stile to climb before joining the road which leads into the village. Turn right here towards the parish church and then left into South Street.

The stone and flint church, dedicated to St Giles, holds a central point in the village where it forms a focus for much of the village activity. With its square turret fringed with pinnacles it was extensively restored by the Victorians, but there are much older artefacts within. One of the earliest fire engines in the country has found a resting place in the north aisle of the church. Its two oldest tombs are of the Bonhams, dating back to the 15th century, and the Grobhams who died in the 17th century.

Look out for the unusual collection of bread stones built into the wall below the churchyard on the street corner. Inscriptions record the price of bread at various times from 1800 and the nearby bakery was only closed in 1982.

Wishford Church

3 Continue along South Street passing pretty thatched cottages and flint houses and the Oak Apple field on the right. Two roads converge at a small green (SU 080 351). This is the home of the Town End Oak, starting point of the Oak Apple procession and resting place for the cut boughs that wait to be judged on Oak Apple Day. For those who are completing the shorter "village-only" circuit turn right along Station Road to return to the *Royal Oak*. A more rural return route can be taken by turning right at the metal barrier found shortly after walking under the railway bridge.

4 A few metres further south from the small green a track leads under the railway line which links Portsmouth with Cardiff or more locally, Salisbury and Warminster. Turn right here under the brick bridge to start the climb to Hadden Hill. The route is signed past a metal barrier and follows a wide grassy, rutted track as it rises out of the valley.

Not far from the summit a well placed wooden bench at the side of the track is a good spot to sit and take in the landmarks across the valley. On clear days there are views to Salisbury Plain with distant tree plantations on the horizon. In the near distance the line of the A303 can be pinpointed by the movement of traffic as flashes of light are reflected off high speed windscreens. Across the valley, on opposite hillsides, field borders curve over the slopes, with isolated barns bearing witness to the agricultural activities which have been carried out over this land for centuries.

OAK APPLE DAY All residents of Great Wishford are entitled to membership of the Oak Apple Club, formed in 1892 to preserve the rights of the villagers to cut wood in Grovely. On 29th May every year these rights are confirmed by Oak Apple Day celebrations which last from dawn to dusk. In keeping with the rights many of the rituals acted out each year are centred round some form of cut wood. An early morning band wakes villagers who rise at dawn to select their bough, which later in the day will be judged. One bough is always raised to the top of the church tower to bring good luck to all who marry during the forthcoming year. Houses in the village are decorated with green branches and small bundles of wood are part of the traditional dance performed outside Salisbury Cathedral where the rights are proclaimed each year. Villagers then return to a formal lunch held in a marquee in the Oak Apple Field. A fancy dress procession through the village follows, lead by a May Queen, and ending up in the Oak Apple field. Dancing, stalls and sideshows are part of the afternoon's entertainment, with the village resting only for a few moments before the evening party begins.

View of Little Wishford and Great Wishford from Hadden Hill and across the Wylye valley

5 At the top of the hill a blue bridleway sign marks the entrance to Grovely Woods (SU 071 344). Continue ahead for some 800m, and then follow the track as it veers left up a slight rise.

On entering the wood your route passes coppiced hazel and oak where bluebells and primroses cover the ground in spring. The excellent level track brings the walker the first sight of the varieties of soft colours seen when columns of tree trunks vanish into the background. Where the track begins its climb it is worth stopping alongside the smooth grey bark of a sturdy beech tree to glance to the left through a gap in the woodland. Walled by the high trees a secluded grassy dip in the hillside draws the eye down to enchanting views over the now distant valley.

6 At the top (SU 065 337) it meets the tarmac surface which runs along the ridge of the hill, on or close to the route of a Roman Road running from the Mendips via Old Sarum to the Southampton area. Turn right on to this level track and follow it westwards.

The track along the ridge, one of the oldest routes in the area, is bordered by a wide green verge, adding a special dignity to the magnificent line of mature beech trees stretching in both directions. You are walking towards what remains of Grovely village. Only a few dwellings stand today but once this small hill-top community had its own school and church. The latter no longer exists, but the bell from its tower is used each year as part of the Oak Apple ceremonies. During World War II the cover of these woods was used for storing ammunition, but today walkers are likely to meet up with nothing more hostile than a timid roe deer crossing their path.

7 Continue along this track until the road turns off to the right (SU 053 342), curving round to the tarmac track leading up to Grovely cottages. Turn right on to this to start the return journey to the valley. After 500m on the downward slope take the track signed as a 'Permissive Path' which forks left off into the woods (at SU 055 343).

Here on the right the dense foliage of tall spruce allows little light to penetrate, while on the left it is still possible to see over the top of the tufted twigs of young larch. Further into the wood the leaf canopy is high and on windy days, although all may be still on the ground, there will be a blustery roar through the swaying treetops above.

8 The path dips and curves but is well signed as it meanders through the woods. There are two possible exits from the permissive path which leave the cover of Grovely to join rights of way crossing Ebsbury Hill. The marker for the first is a large rotting tree stump to the left of the path (at SU 062 352). A right turn here allows a view across to opposite slopes and meets up with a field edge. On emerging from the woods, turn half left and, leaving a lone beech tree on your right, head for the top end of a line of windswept beech. An open metal gate marks the track which runs along the edge of a small copse before meeting up with a Wiltshire gate. Go through the gate and follow the line of the fence to meet up with the sunken track which climbs from the village to Ebsbury (SU 070353).

9 To take the second exit which gives wide views a little higher up the valley continue along the permissive path until it emerges on the hilltop (SU 064 354). Turn right here to cross the grassy banks of an early settlement and meet up with the northern boundary of the small copse.

To the left the line of the Till Valley with the villages of Stapleford and Berwick St James can be seen. Over a row of pine trees the horizon ahead stretches to Beacon Hill above Amesbury and the Hampshire borders beyond. To the east, although the city of Salisbury lies hidden behind hills, its cathedral spire is clearly visible. The walk is across springy turf where larks may be singing high above and buzzards wheeling over Grovely's wooded slopes.

10 At the corner of the field go through the gate (at SU 070 353) to find another bench presenting an opportunity to sit and gaze across the valley. Continue down the track enjoying views of Stoford, South Newton and the rooftops of Wishford. All too visible as well is the stream of traffic along the A36, an unwelcome reminder of the transport burden borne by the Wylye valley. The sunken route that leads off Ebsbury provides easy downhill walking passing the village cemetery before meeting up with Grovely Road. Turn left under the railway bridge to return to our starting point at the *Royal Oak*.

Further Reading

Frampton, George, 1992, *Grovely! Grovely! Grovely! And All Grovely! The history of Oak Apple Day in Great Wishford* (Quacks Books)

Paskin, Marjorie, 1983, *The Parish Church of Wishford Magna* (privately published)

NOTE: Wilton Estate Office provides a map of Permissive Paths through Grovely Woods. The author wishes to acknowledge the help given her by Wilton Estate Office and by fellow walkers.

9 Park (and Walk) and Ride

Riverside Salisbury (6.5 miles/ 10.5km)

by John Chandler   (OS Explorer 130)

There have been many walking guides to Salisbury. This is different, in two ways. It makes use of a newly introduced (2001) park-and-ride facility, to provide a linear walk into and around Salisbury, returning to the start by bus. And it explores, not Salisbury's historic centre (although that is an optional diversion), but its historic suburbs, and the way in which they, and the city, have been affected by its rivers.

The walk begins at the Beehive park-and-ride car park, off the A345 Amesbury road north of Old Sarum. It proceeds via Old Sarum to the riverside walk which leads to the city centre alongside the River Avon. From there it takes the Town Path to Harnham and then climbs on to Harnham Hill for the view over Salisbury, before returning via the Cathedral Close to pick up the park-and-ride bus in New Canal.

The park-and-ride facility does not currently (2002) operate on Sundays or during the evenings. At these times walkers should begin from Old Sarum (there is a convenient lay-by opposite the Old Castle Inn on the A345 when the Old Sarum car park is closed), and catch any of the service buses operating via the A345 towards Amesbury to return. Please check times of Sunday and evening bus services beforehand.

1 Begin at the Beehive Park and Ride facility (SU 145 335) beside the A345 Amesbury road 3km north of central Salisbury (on Sundays, when it is closed, begin at Old Sarum, point 2 below). You must take your ticket with you, but do not catch the park-and-ride bus. Walk out of

the car park in the direction of Old Sarum, and to the left of the roundabout cross the road from the business park. Pick up the broad footpath and cycleway which takes you to the left of the ornate cottage.

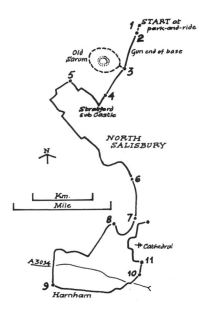

No fewer than five Roman roads converged on Old Sarum, and two (from Silchester and Mildenhall, near Marlborough) meet at the 'Beehive', and survive as important modern roads. The nickname describes the shape of this ornate tollhouse, which was built in about 1830 to house the gatekeeper who collected tolls from travellers on the two turnpike roads, to Marlborough via Tidworth and to Amesbury, which met here.

2 Walk along the footpath beside the main A345 road, noting the 'Gun End of Base' stone and the actual gun barrel sunk in the field behind it. This memorial of the Ordnance Survey's primary triangulation survey of southern England is described on the stone. Continue to the top of the hill, past the vehicle entrance to Old Sarum, until you see a layby on the right opposite the *Old Castle Inn* on the left. Cross with great care the main road here and find the footpath sign to Old Sarum. Optionally you can climb from here by another footpath up into Old Sarum to explore the monument before returning to this point to resume the walk.

OLD SARUM is one of the most impressive and remarkable sites in a county which is hardly lacking in archaeological wonders. In essence it is an iron age (late prehistoric) hillfort, which became a focus for the Roman road network of southern England. It seems then to have been refortified in the Dark Ages, and later maintained in readiness as a citadel for the nearby Saxon town of Wilton. In the 11th and 12th centuries it became a town again in its own right, with a strong Norman castle created within the prehistoric earthworks, and a cathedral perched Durham-like on the hilltop beside it. Much of the town lay outside the defences, and our walk takes us through the probable site of its centre. The decision, implemented in the early 13th century, to move the cathedral to a new site, New Sarum (modern Salisbury) sentenced the old settlement to a lingering death, but it continued as a 'rotten borough' to send members to Parliament until 1832.

3 Follow the footpath along the hedgeline to a metal gate. Do not go through this gate but drop down to the left in front of it into the holloway path, and continue your descent in the holloway. After 300m notice a memorial stone with plaque (sometimes missing through vandalism) marking the site of the Parliament Tree.

Old Sarum was the most blatant of those constituencies which returned members to Parliament until reform in 1832, even though they had in effect no electorate. This privilege reflected its status as a town in the middle ages, and ignored the subsequent exit of its population in favour of New Sarum. Between 1625 and 1831 the number of voters fluctuated between three and ten, whose eligibility depended on their tenure of burgage plots, which were arranged alongside the holloway path we are walking. The stone commemorates the position of the Parliament Tree, cut down in 1905, which was close by the 'electing acre' where the rigged elections had been held. This is therefore a significant place in the history of Parliamentary democracy (or lack of it); but it is also interesting in that it prompts the question, 'Where actually was Old Sarum?' There is growing evidence that the centre of the town of Old Sarum, during the century before its demise, was not in the hillfort, as used to be thought, nor even outside its east gate (around the *Old Castle Inn*), as excavations during the 1960s suggested, but here where the burgage plots were, along the holloway and extending down to a fording or bridging place. In that case the move from Old to New Sarum was not a migration down the hill at all, but a short walk alongside the river similar to that which we are about to undertake.

4 Continue down the hollow for another 300m until it becomes a gravel drive for houses on either side. Look for a footpath between houses on the right, and take this alongside the field behind. At the far end of this field veer slightly left and cross a field diagonally until you meet a track coming down from Old Sarum. Turn left to the road, then right (north) along it for 200m.

It is somewhere around here that Stratford sub Castle begins to shake off the ribbon of suburban housing that has pursued it for a mile and more, all the way up Stratford Road from the city, and starts to become a secluded Woodford valley village. The site of the paved (i.e. Roman) ford from which it is named is uncertain, but the church's presence, in company with the older, more substantial houses, at the northern end of the settlement points to an early crossing here (perhaps near our footbridge), rather than downstream where the road double bends. Stratford's territory was once extensive, and much of Salisbury's northern expansion, such as the Paul's Dene estate, has been built on its former farmland.

5 Cross left and walk down Mill Lane (footpath signed Devizes Road), noting the watermeadows on both sides.

SCAMELL'S BRIDGE Its story is told on two plaques on the bridge itself. It was built in 1857 by a Leeds ironfounder to carry the railway line across nearby Castle Street to where the new railway stations were being constructed at Fisherton. In 1899 the railway bridge was replaced and Thomas Scamell moved it to its present position 'without the aid of any machinery'. At the time new housing estates were springing up on both sides of the river, and the bridge offered the only convenient link between them. It was especially useful as a short cut to the station for residents of the Wyndham Park estate. But Scamell's motive was not philanthropic. The bridge was connected to Nelson Road (now largely disappeared under the ring road), which remained a toll road until bought by the city council in 1930.

At the lane's end the path bears left and crosses the River Avon by a footbridge. Pause here to look back at Old Sarum, and downstream to the cathedral spire (and gasholder). Then, after 200m, at a cross-road of tracks turn left down the valley towards Salisbury. Continue down this path for 800m as far as the allotments, where it bears left to the river and then along the riverbank as a raised duckboard. Keep walking close to the river, and heading past play areas make first for the gasholder, then the fire station. Cross Ashley Road (by the fire station) and keep beside the river. The path skirts Waitrose car park, passes under the city ring road, and arrives at a metal bridge across the river (see box).

6 Do not cross Scamell's Bridge, but keeping the river on your left walk downstream, alongside the coach station and the central car park, until you reach shops and see a brick arch, part of the town mill, ahead. Pass beneath this arch and follow the path until it emerges on a main road (Bridge Street) beside Fisherton Bridge (If you wish you could diverge from the walk here to explore the city and close).

Throughout their history Fisherton Anger (pronounced like 'Ranger') has been Salisbury's most important suburb, and until a few paces before we reached the Maltings shops we have been walking (historically) in Fisherton, not Salisbury. The early centre of Fisherton lay further west, near the railway station and modern St Paul's roundabout, but as Salisbury prospered so Fisherton Street, linking the old village to the city, became a busy if not exactly thriving suburb. By the bridge upstream on the Fisherton side stood a medieval Dominican friary, which was replaced in the 16th century by an inn. Downstream beneath the Victorian clock tower a fragment of the Tudor and later county gaol can be seen, and beyond it the former Salisbury Infirmary, opened in 1771. Inns, shops, chapels and almshouses continue along the street, with the railway stations beyond. The central car park, alongside which we have walked, was until the 1960s occupied by large malthouses, with their own railway line threading between them from the station to the market house (on the site of the present library). The Town or Bishop's Mill is probably on the site of a Saxon (thus pre-city) mill, which was rebuilt when the city began. The present building dates from 1757 and was later used to generate electricity.

7 Cross Bridge Street by the pedestrian crossing and continue by a path alongside the left bank of the river, to a second road bridge, Crane Bridge. Cross this bridge and resume the river walk on the right bank. The path emerges into a public park (Elizabeth Gardens), and you should bear right and walk through it, along one of several paths, until it is narrowed to a point by the road lined with houses on its right. Here a path (signed to Harnham) sets off to the left, crossing the river by a footbridge.

Salisbury Cathedral across the river, from Elizabeth Gardens

8 Take the path to Harnham (known as the Town Path), and follow it across the watermeadows, all the way to Harnham Mill (600m), where refreshments and a famous view of the cathedral are available. Walk along the mill's approach road and at the junction turn right into Middle Street. Continue along this street for 600m, where it bears left and becomes Upper Street, leading to a busy main road (A3094 to Netherhampton). Cross this road with care and take the footpath opposite, Carrion Pond Drove, which runs for 300m behind gardens to bring you to former chalk pits at the foot of an escarpment.

Harnham Mill, a corn mill and later a fulling mill for cloth, retains some of its early masonry, and has the pleasing 'pepper and salt work' of flint and stone chequers characteristic of the south Wiltshire valleys. It straddles one course of the River Nadder (incorporating since Wilton the River Wylye also), which a little downstream from here flows into the Avon.

9 At the chalk pits turn left through the bars and make your way diagonally up the hillside to reach the path which runs along close to the hilltop. After some 300m this becomes part of the designated Avon Valley Path, but

continues on the same course. It is known as the Bishop's Walk because, as a plaque explains, it was given to the city by a Victorian bishop of Salisbury. Eventually the path descends by steps to join the Old Blandford Road at the end of a modern cul de sac, Grasmere Close. Continue down to the main road and, crossing it with care, bear right then left into Harnham Road, past a row of white cottages on your right. This road ends at traffic lights, and bear left on to Harnham Bridge.

By descending from the Old Blandford Road to Harnham Bridge you are following in the footsteps of the medieval traveller from the west country towards London. Here one bridge (in two parts) takes you over the combined rivers of Wylye, Nadder and Avon which, until it was built in 1244, you would have had to tackle separately, at Wilton and Old Sarum. It also leads you into Salisbury, and so has always offered commercially minded citizens the chance to profit (at Wilton's expense) from the passing trade. There was a ford here prior to the bridge, and the twin settlements of Harnham, East and West, already existed. The *Rose and Crown* hotel, which wraps itself pleasingly into the bend, retains 14th-century work in its north range (nearer the bridge) and 16th-century work in the south range. Harnham Bridge was widened in 1774, and carried all southbound traffic from the city until 1933.

Harnham Mill

10 **Cross Harnham bridge and continue as far as the Close Wall ahead of you, noting the following buildings of interest.**

Most people miss the former St John's Chapel, which stands on the island between the two parts of Harnham Bridge, looking like the Regency dwelling into which it was converted. But glance below bridge level and you will see blocked medieval pointed windows and a doorway. The chapel was built at the same time as the bridge, in the 1240s. Of similar date is the much more obvious St Nicholas's Hospital, a substantial almshouse complex which retains many medieval features. This is on your right, and beyond it on the left, set back from the road, is a much altered and disguised fragment of Salisbury's failed medieval university, De Vaux College. The building on the corner, sporting the arms of Oxford University, is De Vaux House, and this too contains medieval fabric from the college.

11 **This rather unconventional walk around Salisbury ends by passing without comment the places which most visitors come to see, and which most guidebooks describe. At the Close wall turn left, along De Vaux Place, and enter the Close by Harnham Gate. Turn right, walk past the west front of the cathedral and straight ahead to leave by the High Street gate. Walk along High Street, crossing one set of traffic lights into the pedestrianised section. Turn right into New Canal, and you will find the Park and Ride bus stop after about 150m. Buses run back to the Beehive frequently throughout the day.**

Further Reading

Chandler, John, 1983, *Endless Street: a history of Salisbury and its people* (Hobnob Press)

Chandler, John, 1992, *Salisbury: history and guide* (Alan Sutton) [includes walking tours of the city and close]

Newman, Ruth, and Howells, Jane 2001, *Salisbury past* (Phillimore)

Victoria History of Wiltshire, vol. 6, 1962 [includes histories of Stratford sub Castle and Fisherton, as well as Old Sarum and Salisbury]

10 In Royal Footsteps

Clarendon Revisited

(5 mile / 8km linear route, or circuits, various lengths)

by Victoria Coombes   (OS Explorer 130, 131)

Following ancient pathways this walk takes in the romantic ruins of a royal hunting lodge and medieval palace. It travels through the magnificent scenery of parkland on the eastern borders of the county with views across the city of Salisbury to the south and farmland to the north. Along the way the walker will meet deer and pheasant beside their path while buzzards soar overhead. In summer the call of the chiff-chaff and cuckoo joins the song of blackbirds and robins in the woods. Most of the route follows broad tracks with one or two short climbs, but there are no stiles. The walk allows various options as a linear route or circuits of different lengths, and passes through the village of Pitton, where there is a pub and a shop, and which may be used as a starting point for the shortest circuit. This text will cover the longest route allowing walkers to take their pick according to energy or time available. The options are:

15 km/10 mile circuit starting from Salisbury's city centre

12 km/8 mile circuit starting from the edge of the Clarendon Estate

7 km/4.5 mile circuit starting from the village of Pitton.

As an 8 km/5 mile linear route along part of the Clarendon Way, a 26 mile official walk from Salisbury to Winchester. This means either using the bus service between Pitton and Salisbury or walking with friends and leaving a car at one end.

1 **Start from Salisbury Market Square (SU 144 300) and leave the city centre by facing the Guildhall and walking to the left of it (Queen Street). Turn left at the junction**

into Milford Street, passing the *Red Lion* hotel on your right, and continue straight on beneath the ring road flyover at traffic lights. Continue straight on up Milford Hill, using the separate tree lined pathway on the left which lifts walkers above the traffic.

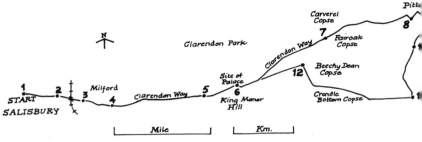

This is one of the city's ancient highways. In his book *Endless Street*, John Chandler describes this street as one of the earliest routes into Salisbury. And in his booklet on *Clarendon Palace*, Tom James suggests that the fact that there was already an established track between the abbey at Wilton and the Palace might well have provided a good reason for the siting of New Salisbury when it moved from Old Sarum. I like this idea and now think of the first part of this walk as an early section of the London to Exeter road, or part of a medieval A30 or A303.

2 At the top of Milford Hill you reach the red brick buildings of the Godolphin School (SU 151 299), a substantial landmark. Leaving the school on the left, follow the ancient sunken route into Milford Hollow, a name recorded in a city survey as long ago as 1274.

Before crossing the bridge over the Southampton to Salisbury railway line it is worth noticing the two houses on the left bank. Legend has it that one of these was once an inn at which travellers would stop to tidy themselves before entering the cathedral city. In the tiny patch of woodland on the far side of the bridge nuthatches and treecreepers sometimes join families of long tailed tits.

3 At the bottom of the hill continue ahead into Milford Mill Road, passing the grey stone pile of Milford Manor on the right and its attractive chequerboard wall of flint and stone. The road crosses two channels of the River Bourne over a pretty medieval stone bridge, one of the first river crossings into the city. Without changing direction, continue up Queen Manor Road (SU 158 297).

The medieval bridge which crosses the River Bourne at Milford

This is another sunken route and at the top of the hill there are good views across the eastern fringes of Salisbury and the Avon valley. Trees on top of the hillfort distinguish Clearbury Ring on the skyline and the buildings of Salisbury District Hospital spread across the opposite hillside. After this point, urban development is left behind as the lane winds past fields to meet the gates of the 5,000-acre Clarendon Park Estate, home of the Christie-Miller family since 1919. For those who have driven out of the town there is enough space here for one or two cars to be left.

4 **Walk through the gates where a post carries a sign (bishop's mitre) for the Clarendon Way and another (spire between hills) for the Sarum Way. After passing farm buildings the level tarmac track runs between fields which gently slope away on either side. After several hundred metres take a well-signed right turn to cross the field diagonally (SU 170 299). At the far side turn right onto a rutted track winding up the hill**

This is the land of the yellow hammer, a small bunting often seen singing its supposed song of 'a little bit of bread and no cheese' from the heights of telegraph wires which break up the smooth horizontal lines of this large field. In summer delicate pink cups of wild rose arch out from the high tangled hedgerows and grassy banks are a sea of chalkland flowers. If the walker is in need of a breather half way up the hill, look out for the viewpoint sign on the right hand bank, where a level plateau is home to early purple orchids.

5 The track hairpins back to the right, climbing steeply to a picnic bench and table bringing a chance to sit and drink in the scenery. Continue to the top of the hill.

Here a white thatched house, King Manor Cottage, stands in splendid isolation with only the nearby ruins of a palace providing the ghost of a neighbour. The historic site of Clarendon Palace lies behind this cottage and a kissing gate at either end of the fenced site allows walkers to divert their path to visit the ruins.

6 To visit the site turn left before King Manor Cottage (SU 182 302) and enter through a kissing gate. The exit is at the far side through another gate allowing walkers to return to the Clarendon Way. Continue along the ridge of the hill for 400m and take the signed turning left into the woods (SU 185 302).

CLARENDON PALACE There has been continuous settlement on this site since the Neolithic period. Prehistoric cemeteries and flint scatters in the plough give evidence of 6,000 years of habitation. The fence encloses part of what was once the largest medieval deer park in England and the site of the ruins of Clarendon Palace, which was occupied throughout the middle ages. Documentary history gives evidence of a visit by William the Conqueror and the last recorded royal visit was by Queen Elizabeth I in 1574. Originally no more than a hunting box, Henry III promoted it to be one of the major palaces in England. Samples of the tiled floors and pottery found at the site can be seen in Salisbury and South Wiltshire Museum and the British Museum.

In 1998 a five-year plan was set up to halt the damage being caused by trees, vegetation and neglect. The site has been fenced and a small flock of sheep introduced to keep the vegetation down. Some replacements are taking place within structures in order to conserve and consolidate the ruins. Dr T B James, who is leading this work, explains that one of the aims is to make the site more legible. It has certainly made it more accessible. Five years ago the ruins were hidden in dense woodland and invisible from the passing Right of Way.

In spring on either side of this pathway a misty haze of bluebells spreads beneath the coppiced hazel. The path is well signed and runs through extensive woodland where it is hard to believe the city centre is only a few miles away. Roe deer, grey squirrels and wood pigeon will be the most likely fellow creatures to share this sheltered landscape, where the trees create ever changing patterns of light and shade. The path crosses several tracks as it continues straight ahead on level ground.

All that remains standing of the eastern wall of Clarendon's Great Hall

7 Soon after the plantings change to conifers, with Fairoak Copse to the right and Carverel Copse on the left, the path starts to wind down the hillside, opening up on one side. At the bottom of the hill it meets up with a tarmac track beside farm buildings and opposite a line of four white cottages. Leaving these on your right, follow the signed route straight ahead and continue along a narrow path under the shelter of conifers to emerge by a large beech tree. The path ahead runs between fields as it heads towards Pitton School. Turn right round the edge of the field to meet up with a tarmac road beside the pumping station. (SU 210 312).

8 Turn left to reach Pitton village street and enjoy a short spell of easier walking after the rough woodland tracks. At this point our route parts from the official Clarendon Way which continues straight ahead towards West Winterslow. At the crossroads turn right up Whitehill. A Wesleyan Chapel dated 1888 sits against the road on the right and on the left the low white building of the *Silver Plough* stands back from the road. This is the starting point for those who have chosen the shortest circuit, or the finishing point for those who have simply walked out to Pitton from Salisbury.

9 Just past the village hall, turn right where a faded sign *'Private road – footpath only'* marks the turning SU 213 312. At the far end of the tennis court look out for a small arrow sign on a hedge. Turn left here to follow a narrow footpath running parallel with the track.

The path runs behind a pretty brick and flint cottage and is bridged by three fallen trees as it climbs steeply through woods. At the top of the hill it emerges from what is obviously a well-trodden pathway on a well-loved route to reach open pasture. A short way along a bench has been placed in memory of Jack Judd 1921–1994 and in spring daffodils decorate this spot. I can

PITTON The village lies five miles to the east of Salisbury and nestles in the folds of the South Wiltshire downs. It was once the home of that well loved writer on the countryside, Ralph Whitlock. A short circuit round the village will take in the pretty flint church of St Peter and the possibility of buying refreshment at the village shop. The *Silver Plough* run by Carol and Adrian Clifton welcomes walkers and are happy to share their car parking facilities. The pub has become well known for its good home cooking and offers a wide range of dishes from Ploughman's to À La Carte. Outside tables in a south facing garden are popular in good weather.

never resist a short rest here giving time to admire views across to the wooded slopes and appreciate the practical memorial.

10 Continue in the same direction to the corner of the field where several tracks meet (SU 209 305). Take the route ahead winding into the woods with fields on the left. At one point this rutted track sometimes becomes a wide lake and a bypass has been created through adjoining woods to avoid its muddy depths.

Look out here for an unusual evergreen bush (about 25-80cm high) with straight stalks growing from a central point. These clumps are *Butcher's broom* – a popular plant with florists for its year-round foliage. What look like perfectly formed, dark green leaves are in fact flattened stems. The path runs through a wide mix of trees - oak, beech, holly, yew, chestnut and ash, many with twisted lengths of Traveller's-joy climbing high into their branches.

Hawthorn blossom lines the route looking back along the edge of Beechy Dean Copse

11 After a few hundred metres look out for a stile on the left which marks the point to turn right (SU 210 298). The path is signed and continues a short way through more woodland now heading westwards back to Salisbury. As it leaves the wood it dips down between fields, crossing a farm track then gently rising to return to the cover of trees beside a patch of teasels. With spruce plantations on the left and beech on the right the track arrives at an estate road. Cross over the tarmac track and continue past

Crendle Bottom Copse towards a large, open, prairie-sized field. Turn right here, passing Beechy Dean Copse on the right, to climb back to the ridge at the top of the hill and follow round the edge of the field by turning left (SU 192 304).

12 After 600m the track meets up again with the point we left earlier (SU 185 302) to complete the Pitton circuit. For those who started at Pitton and want to include the Palace ruins, continue along the track before returning to this point and following earlier directions from this point. For those who began at the Salisbury end, continue the return journey on an easy downhill route back to the city with good views of the cathedral spire on the way.

Further Reading

James, Tom B, 1988, *Clarendon: a medieval royal palace* (Salisbury and South Wiltshire Museum)
Whitlock, Ralph, 1988, *Letters from an English Village* (Ex Libris)

NOTE: The author wishes to acknowledge the help given her by Prof Tom Beuamont James (King Alfred's, Winchester), the Clarendon Estate Office, and her fellow walkers.

11 Another Avon for Shakespeare

Downton and the Avon Valley Path

(4 miles/ 6.5 km)

by Chris Cole   (OS Explorer 130)

At the southern gateway to Wiltshire, this easy walk follows a dramatic stretch of one of England's great rivers. The Avon Valley is protected from the threats of modern development and offers a safe habitat for an extensive range of wildlife. Ancient history combines with local industry to make Downton an interesting village to explore, and as well as examining its origins we shall relive episodes from its more recent past. Walking is on minor roads, hard tracks, and riverside paths. The terrain is level but can be muddy in places, and it should be borne in mind that when the river is in flood some sections of the route will be impassable. Refreshments, shops, and other facilities are available in Downton, and The Moot car park is well signposted from the junction of the A338 and B3080.

1 Start at the free car park in Moot Lane, Downton, and walk up Moot Lane the short distance to the B3080 (SU 182 215). Turn left and follow the main road through the village. After the *King's Arms* take a detour to inspect the church, then continue to the old tannery (SU 180 215).

> See how this river comes me cranking in,
> And cuts me from the best of all my land . . .
> (*Henry IV, Part 1*)

If you did not know better, you could be forgiven for thinking that Shakespeare was born in Wiltshire. After all, two of the county's

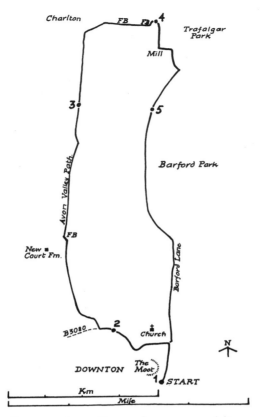

rivers bear the name Avon. No wonder overseas visitors are often
confused to find that Stratford is somewhere else entirely.

But you will not be confused by this walk, unless the river is
in flood, for our route takes us directly across the floodplain,
and is therefore waterlogged at certain times of the year.
Indeed, flooding has been a major hazard for Downton, not least
in December 2000 after Britain's wettest autumn on record.
Thankfully, such extreme flood levels occur only rarely, and
recent modifications to the various river channels should
alleviate future disasters.

Historically, Downton has a long pedigree. After the last Ice
Age ended around 12,000 years ago, herds of wild animals began
to graze in the lush water meadows, attracting primitive
hunters, some of whom sailed north–south along the Avon,
whilst others took advantage of a natural ford that enabled
them to travel east–west across the river valley. Downton
therefore became a crossroads, one which ironically would make
it vulnerable to subsequent flooding.

The discovery of many flint tools dates the earliest
settlements to around 5,000 BC. The Romans occupied the area

for a time, leaving behind the remains of a villa. At some point a large earthwork was created to defend the village, first by the Saxons, then by the Normans who adopted it as the foundations of one of the largest ringwork and bailey castles in England. The map refers to it as motte and bailey, although the difference is so slight that even the experts have difficulty telling them apart.

We shall examine The Moot in greater detail at the end of our walk, which begins as we join the Avon Valley Path along the main road through the village. More history awaits at the flint and stone church of St. Laurence, also of Norman origin, although an earlier church was built here in AD 638 by St. Birinus, the first Bishop of the West Saxons. The church was a powerful force in medieval times, owning and controlling vast areas of land and property. The local Bishop of Winchester was said to be the richest man in England during the 15th century.

It was one of his predecessors, Peter de Roches, who created the borough of Downton in 1209, allowing a thriving industrial community to become established, covering such trades as lace, paper, brewing, bacon and fishing. Farming, like everywhere else, was regularly affected by the weather and prevailing economic conditions. Bad harvests in the 14th century caused the price of corn to escalate and land to become scarce at a time when the whole country was being devastated by the Black Death. Nevertheless, Downton survived and recovered, but when depression once again forced agricultural labourers out of work five centuries later, 10% of the local population emigrated to Canada as part of a mass exodus sponsored by the parish.

Unlike many villages, the present church does not occupy a commanding position where it can dominate the skyline. Instead, the eye is drawn instinctively to a more modern building that has become a prominent feature of the Downton landscape. Tanning was introduced to Downton 800 years ago, and had grown into a significant industry by the 19th century. In 1919 an impressive new tannery was built alongside the mill stream that supplied power through a large waterwheel. For many years the Downton Tanning Company was an important local employer, but competition from cheaper imports forced the business to close its doors in 1998. Fortunately the building has survived and is being converted to retirement housing.

What, man! more water glideth by the mill . . . (*Titus Andronicus*)

Here, then, is our first encounter with the Avon as it flows past the tannery, under the road, then alongside former mill properties as it approaches the Hampshire county boundary, and eventually enters the sea at Christchurch. Rising in the Vale of Pewsey, the river falls 150 metres over its 48 mile course, draining an area of 1,132 square miles. After meandering slowly through the landscape north of Salisbury, its character changes as it merges with the Bourne, Nadder and Ebble, to create a broad lower valley of meadows and pastures through which the river splits up into several different channels.

2 **Continue along the main road as far as the second river bridge (SU 175 215) where a signpost reads Charlton All Saints 1½ miles. Go right alongside the cottage and follow the riverside path, gradually moving away from the main channel. Cross a footbridge by New Court Farm and turn right on to a concrete road as far as a farm gateway where a stile leads into a field on the right (SU 176 226).**

> . . . not only the most beautiful but the most important, for after all, the Salisbury Avon is the river into which all the others pour and which continues, like the broad arm of this outstretched hand, as it journeys to the sea.   (Pamela Street, *Portrait of Wiltshire*)

As the village recedes behind us the countryside begins. Initially it may be just horses grazing in the adjacent field, or Bewick's

Swan on River Avon near Charlton All Saints

swans drifting gracefully on the fast flowing current, but be prepared for a wider selection of wildlife as you venture further up the valley. According to English Nature the Avon has '. . . a greater range of habitat diversity and a more diverse flora and fauna than any other chalk river in Britain'.

Some animal species may be hidden, or scurry for cover as you approach, but not the herons. Perched in trees or circling overhead, they are safe from human interference and your passing will not detract them from the main reason they are here. The exceptional quality of the water makes the Avon ideal for fishing. Twenty-four species of fish have been recorded, including barbel and salmon. What better location for a fish farm. And where there are fish, expect to find herons, lots of them.

3 After leaving the concrete road cross the next two fields, pass the fish farm, and aim for the houses at Charlton. Cross the gravel track by the two stiles (SU 177 237) and veer right over the next field, through a gap in the hedge, then look for two footbridges beyond the bushes.

At the tiny village of Charlton All Saints we leave the Avon Valley Path as it enters the final leg of its 34 mile journey. This long distance footpath follows the general direction of the river between Christchurch and Salisbury, and is waymarked by green arrows enclosing a bridge symbol. During the 17th century various attempts were made to transform the Avon into a fully navigable waterway, with the intention that Salisbury would become a port to rival Bristol. An Act of Parliament sanctioned an improvement scheme but funds ran out and the work came to a halt in 1677. When it was revived eight years later, short sections of canal were cut to bypass the main river, but it is doubtful whether the waterway was ever fully navigable for large vessels. Since the plan was finally abandoned in 1730 the only regular traffic has been the constant turnover of birds and wildfowl. After crossing the first river channel our route passes the reedbeds which lapwings, redshanks and snipe treat as one of their key spring feeding grounds. Elsewhere, geese, ducks and swans are regularly seen, and as we cross their territory we must be especially careful not to disturb them. Take binoculars by all means, but leave the dog at home, or at least keep it on a short lead.

4 Cross the river and follow the footpath over the floodplain, being careful not to stray into the reedbeds. Cross three weirs, taking care if the boards are wet, go left in front of the millhouse (SU 182 235), then uphill on a concrete track. Fork right at the top to pass a derelict church, then right again around the last house and through the gateway (SU 183 234).

Main Weir, River Avon, Trafalgar Park

What dreadful noise of waters in mine ears! (*Richard III*, Act 1)

The main weir is impressive and will not fail to capture your attention. You may want to rest here awhile to absorb the atmosphere, especially in autumn when the trees are a kaleido-scope of colour. The millhouse and derelict church mark our entry into Trafalgar Park. Amongst the trees stands a fine mansion built in 1733 for a city banker. Originally called Standlynch House, it was renamed in 1814 when presented to Lord Nelson's heirs in honour of the Admiral's famous victory. Subsequently sold in 1948, it gradually fell into disuse, but is now being renovated by the present owner who recognises its importance as part of the nation's architectural heritage. The Trafalgar name is also associated with the fish farm which produces 900 tons of trout annually, making it the largest of its kind in the country – and probably the largest gathering of herons, with whom we renew our acquaintance as we pass by on the opposite side.

5 Follow the wide track across the field past Trafalgar Fisheries and Barford Park Farm. Emerging onto Barford Lane (SU 182 222) go straight ahead to enter Downton opposite Moot Lane.

Our final stroll back into Downton parallels the tree-lined route of the old Salisbury & Dorset Joint Railway. When Countess

The Mill Pond, Trafalgar Park

Nelson performed the opening ceremony at Downton station bells rang out in Salisbury to mark the event. But the celebrations were short-lived, for in 1884 it became the setting for Britain's worst railway accident up to that time. Excessive speed and poor track maintenance derailed a train south of Downton station, killing five passengers, and injuring many more. The *Illustrated London News* published pictures of the wrecked train, its flimsy carriages scattered alongside the embankment at Pile Bridge on the county boundary (SU 174 202).

During its 98-year history it was never a busy line, but it did serve a useful purpose by bringing many special trains to festivals at The Moot, which by this time had become a landscaped garden. As the 20th century dawned The Moot was a regular venue for fêtes and concerts. Shakespeare plays were especially popular. In 1908 a certain Miss Sybil Thorndike appeared here in *The Comedy of Errors*, first performed in 1594 at London's Gray's Inn, for which it had been specifically requested in view of its reputation as a lively farce.

In 1988 The Moot Preservation Trust was formed to restore the 8-acre site. Finish your walk by exploring the network of paths around the ancient earthworks and down to the banks of the river. This may not be Shakespeare's Avon, but I'm sure he would have approved.

Further Reading

Waymouth, David 1999, *Downton: 7000 years of an English Village* (Downton Millennium Book Fund).

12 'A Desperate Pleasant Place'

Vernditch Chase and the Ox Drove Ridgeway (6 miles / 9.6 km)

by Ken Watts   (OS Explorer 118 or 130)

A testament to the beauty of the countryside to be seen on this walk was recorded by William Chafin, the historian of Cranborne Chase, when he related in 1818 the story of the Chase keeper who, after hearing a parson describing paradise, offered his opinion that paradise seemed to be 'a desperate pleasant place', but that 'if there was a good trout stream running down Chicken Grove Bottom, Fernditch Lodge would beat it out and out'. For my own part I find Vernditch – which was formerly part of Cranborne Chase and lies at the southern extremity of Wiltshire adjoining both Dorset and Hampshire – one of the lesser-known but great delights of Wiltshire, and I try to visit Vernditch at least once every spring at the time when bluebells carpet the woods, nightingales sing from its thickets, and buzzards are frequently seen soaring overhead. This walk, which is associated with three Wiltshire Wildlife Trust Nature Reserves at Chickengrove Bottom, Middleton Down, and Knowle Down, crosses Vernditch Chase and then follows two ancient traffic routes, first part of the Roman road from Badbury Rings in Dorset to Old Sarum, with panoramic views over Dorset and Hampshire, and then the Ox Drove ridgeway with its splendid views north to the parallel Ebble–Nadder ridge, which carried the Salisbury Way turnpike road. The walk is associated with the Elizabethan poet and courtier Sir Philip Sidney, and with John Aubrey, the gossipy Wiltshire biographer and antiquary. The walking throughout is easy on well-defined routes with no steep hills, but as the walk is in remote countryside away from all villages refreshment must be carried if required or obtained before or after the walk. There is a public house (The Queen's Head) at Broad Chalke about three miles from the start point. The walk may be extended by optional diversions into the adjoining Nature Reserves.

1 Begin the walk from Cow Down Hill at SU 023 216, one mile (1.6km) south of Bowerchalke on the south side of Marleycombe Hill near the county boundary with Dorset. Cow Down Hill is approached from Bowerchalke in the Ebble Valley by driving through Misselfore and up the beautiful winding Cross Bottom which is, as are many of the downlands slopes in this area, profusely sprinkled with cowslips in spring. Park beside the Ox Drove and walk 300 metres south-east down the minor road, and where the road turns sharp right at Cutler's Corner (on the county boundary at SU 025 214) leave the road and follow the track on the left which runs at first eastwards down the county boundary along the north edge of Chettle Head Copse. About 700 metres from Cutler's Corner the woods of Vernditch Chase are entered at a place known as Kitt's Grave (SU 031 212), probably because a suicide was buried here on the parish and county boundary. According to the Wiltshire writer Ralph Whitlock this was a girl who drowned herself in a well at Bowerchalke. Continue by swinging a little east of south down a track through woodland with open glades for a little over half a mile (1km) until Vernditch Chase ends at the Roman road (2) at SU 036 203 near the A354.

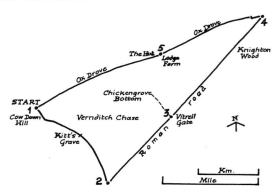

Vernditch Chase as it survives today is a mere remnant of the former Vernditch. When Cranborne Chase extended almost to Wilton its Vernditch Chase was much larger. The 1773 map by Andrews and Dury shows the whole area within the circuit of this walk (that is to the left of walkers) wooded, and designates

Vernditch Chase, where Sidney wrote part of *Arcadia*

it Vernditch Chase. The name derives from 'fern ditch', meaning bracken ditch, as the ancient Grim's Ditch runs through the middle of Vernditch, Grim being an alternative name for the Saxon god Odin or Wodin. Vernditch was neglected and might have been lost had it not been acquired before the Second World War by the composer Balfour Gardiner (1877–1950) who, with his nephew the pioneer environmentalist Rolf Gardiner (1902–71), planted millions of trees on Cranborne Chase in an attempt to recreate the historic landscape. Rolf Gardiner recorded how: 'During a period of forty years, first Balfour, at my instigation, and then I alone planted some three million trees on the chalk downs and among the hazel coppices of this impoverished north-west district of Cranborne Chase. We altered the whole configuration of the landscape'. As a result of these activities the one-inch Ordnance Survey for a time gave Vernditch Chase the alternative name 'Gardiner Forest'. As you emerge from the woods at the Roman road (2) the view ahead is over Bokerley Dyke (here the boundary between Dorset and Hampshire) and over Martin Down Nature Reserve and Pentridge, where the Dorset dialect poet William Barnes (1801–86) was brought up by an aunt and uncle. A mile (1.6km) south-west of this point (2) is Woodyates Inn on the A354, once run by Thomas Browning (1721–94) the great-grandfather of the poet Robert Browning. At Woodyates Inn in 1685 the Duke of Monmouth in his flight after Sedgemoor disguised himself as a shepherd shortly before being captured in Hampshire and taken to London to be executed. Two miles (3.2km) to the east is Martin in Hampshire, the home of the shepherd of W H Hudson's classic Wiltshire book *A Shepherd's Life, Impressions of the South Wiltshire Downs*

(1910), Martin having until boundary adjustments in 1895 been in Wiltshire.

2 Follow the the Roman road with its pronounced *agger* (raised bank) for a mile (1.6km) north-east along the county boundary to Vitrell Gate (3) at SU 046 215 where the minor road from Martin's Drove End to Broad Chalke crosses the Roman road. It is best to walk along the crown of the *agger*, otherwise the fine views into the woodland of Vernditch are missed.

SIR PHILIP SIDNEY (1554–86), the Elizabethan courtier and poet, frequented Vernditch Chase in the year 1580 during which he was out of favour at court as a result of opposing Queen Elizabeth's proposed catholic marriage, and stayed at Wilton House with his sister Mary Countess of Pembroke (1561–1621). For much of this time in Wiltshire he amused himself by writing his verse romance *Arcadia* while riding over the vast Pembroke estates, particularly in Vernditch Chase. John Aubrey (1626–97), who lived only about 3 miles (4.8km) north of Vernditch, tells us that Sidney: 'was wont, when hunting on our pleasant plaines, to take his Table booke out of his pocket, and write downe his notions as they came into his head, when he was writing *Arcadia* (which was never finished by him) . . . These Romancy Plaines, and Boscages did no doubt conduce to the heightening of Sir Philip Sidney's Phansie'. Although Sidney considered *Arcadia* 'but a trifle' it became the most popular work of fiction for a hundred and fifty years after its composition. Such popularity is now difficult to comprehend, a fact debated by that fine poetry critic Edward Thomas when in 1914 he wrote: '. . . we should like to know, why and how *Arcadia* and similar books appealed to the men and women of England from 1590 to 1630, during which ten editions were called for. What kind of truth and beauty they saw in it; what part of humanity was moved by it; whether they detected the influence of Wilton and Salisbury Plain'. Milton considered *Arcadia* 'vain and amatorious', Hazlitt considered it 'one of the greatest monuments to the abuse of intellectual power upon record', and in more recent times T. S. Eliot described it as: 'a monument of dullness'.

3 From Vitrell Gate an optional short diversion (which adds about a mile to the walk) may be made north-west up the road and through a gate on the left (SU 044 216) to visit the Chickengrove Bottom Nature Reserve, a steeply sloped florally rich chalkland reserve which adjoins the woodlands of Vernditch Chase. Return to Vitrell Gate (3) and continue for another mile and a half (2.4km) north-east along the Roman road as it follows the north-west edge of Knighton Wood. The walk may, if required, be shortened by taking one of the rights-of-way north to the Ox Drove from Vitrell Gate (3) or Moody's Gore.

This Roman road is part of the road from Old Sarum to Badbury Rings in Dorset. When following it south-west from Knighton Wood Mr Ivan Margary wrote in *Roman Roads in Britain* (first published 1955): 'It is impossible to exaggerate, and indeed difficult adequately to describe, the magnificence which now lies ahead. For mile after mile, up hill and down, practically all the way to Badbury Rings, the road is seen (and well seen, for much of it is in open downland) as an enormous *agger* over 40 feet wide, sometimes 50 feet, and high in proportion – One feels that one must be viewing the embankment of an abandoned main-line railway rather than a Roman road!'.

4 At the north end of Knighton Wood at SU 062 232 turn left (west) from the Roman road and follow the Ox Drove approximately west past Lodge Farm and The Hut (5) at SU 043 225.

The Ox Drove is an old ridgeway traffic route along which cattle were driven out of the west country past Salisbury and generally on to the London markets, to supply London after its population grew too large to subsist from its own neighbourhood. Droveways tended to avoid turnpikes to evade paying tolls, and when walking these remote and now peaceful old droveways it is easy to imagine them in their heyday when droves of two hundred half-maddened long-horned cattle were urged eastwards by mounted drovers with dogs. On the Ox Drove opposite Knighton Wood we are in John Aubrey Country, because half a mile (0.8km) west of Knighton Wood Farm a very pleasant way called Church Bottom runs north (with beside it Middleton Down Nature Reserve), and after gently descending for a mile and a half (2.5km) enters Broad Chalke beside the site of Manor Farm. Aubrey inherited this farm from his father, but soon lost it with the rest of his inheritance, because he became too engrossed with his literary and archaeological interests to look after his financial affairs – which in his own memorable words 'went Kim-Kam'. This expression is a variant on the expression 'Clean cam', meaning to go entirely awry; it is used by Shakespeare in *Coriolanus*.

A little over a mile (1.6km) along the Ox Drove from (4) Lodge Farm and The Hut (5) are passed.

Lodge Farm, on the south side of the Ox Drove, takes its name from Vernditch Lodge to its south. It has been sensitively reconstructed. The Hut (or its predecessor on the site) was, as were the other 'huts' on old traffic ways in south Wiltshire, an establishment which offered refreshment to travellers and drovers. When poaching was rife in Cranborne Chase The Hut in the 17th century became a rendezvous for gentlemen poachers, for it was not only the poor who poached. Many gentlemen regarded The Chase deer as fair game, and William Chafin in his *Anecdotes of Cranborne Chase* (1818) related how The Hut was a public house, where an apparently respectable musical club met under the pretence of performing music, with the ulterior motive of poaching deer. From the heights of the Ox Drove they would observe where the deer lay up in the copses during the day, set their snares, and in the evening at dusk when the coast was clear return with a cart and bring home their venison. Their leader was a Mr Henry Good, who came from a well-respected family long established at Bower Chalke. By 1773 The Hut was an 'Inoculation House'.

Harry Good, deer-hunter of Cranborne Chase, with accomplices

MIDDLETON DOWN NATURE RESERVE is a fine species-rich chalk downland reserve which lies immediately north of the Ox Drove and west of Church Bottom. It is run by Wiltshire Wildlife Trust, is accessible through a pedestrian gate on the west side of Church Bottom about 150 metres north of the Ox Drove, and is of particular interest in early May for its cowslips and early purple orchids.

5 From The Hut complete the walk by continuing approximately west for almost a mile and a half (2.4km) along the Ox Drove. Cross the Broad Chalke to Martin road (known as Howgare Road) and pass south of Wiltshire Wildlife Trust's Knowle Down Nature Reserve in its steep coombe (SU 032 226) to the start point at Cow Down Hill.

Further Reading

Watts, K, 1998, *Exploring Historic Wiltshire: Volume 2, South*, chapter 11 (Ex Libris Press)

13 Ebble Villages

Broadchalke, Bowerchalke and Fifield Bavant (5.5 miles / 9 km)

by Rex and Sheila Sawyer   (OS Explorer 118 or 130)

The Ebble is the most southerly of the south Wiltshire river valleys and joins the Avon at Salisbury to continue its journey to the sea at Christchurch. This walk lies beneath the beautiful chalk downland fringing the border of Wiltshire with Dorset. From Broadchalke, evolved from prehistoric settlements, it follows an ancient sheep track, with clear views of the surrounding countryside, and at Knowle Farm past an SSSI (Site of Special Scientific Interest) noted for its downland flora and fauna. From the picturesque village of Bowerchalke, for many years the home of the Nobel Prize winner William Golding, the walk encounters further magnificent views of south Wiltshire as we cross to the remains of the hamlet of Fifield Bavant. From here we follow the valley of the Ebble back to Broadchalke, where refreshments may be obtained at the Queen's Head.

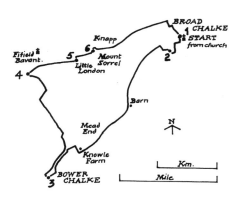

1 Start at the car park behind Broadchalke church (SU 041 254). (Alternatively, you may use the car park at the rear of the *Queen's Head* if you are using their facilities). Leave the car park by the small entrance on to the path and turn left. At the road turn right and almost immediately left, and follow the road to the top. Turn right and, shortly, right again on to a track (SU 039 251).

On the right of the track you can see the side view of Reddish House, once the home of Cecil Beaton, the famous 20th-century cultural figure, society photographer and diarist. More recently it was the home of the pop star Toyah Wilcox.

2 Continue to follow the track around the field on the left and walk for about two miles south-westerly along the track beneath the chalk downland until you enter the farmyard of Knowle Farm. Ignoring the farm dogs (who will seem intimidating but aren't!) follow right around the barn and continue to the main Bowerchalke road. Turn left here (with care). A little way along, opposite Costers Lane (SU 022 234), you will see a track on the left. Follow this around the back of the village (ignoring the main track to your left) until you reach the graveyard (SU 019 230), a good stopping place for refreshment.

BOWERCHALKE The village lies along a spur of the main Ebble Valley road beneath the elegant sweep of chalk downland known as Marleycombe. The village name of Bower, (or Burghe) Chalk is believed to derive from the family of John Atte Burghe who possessed the land in 1456. It was once part of the 'outer ring' of Cranborne Chase and thus subject to the harsh Chase poaching laws. From 1878–1924 the modest Chilmark stone vicarage next to the church was the home of the Rev Edward Collett who, remarkably, printed a *Parish Paper* for over forty years on his own printing press. Copies of this small bulletin were sold to parishioners for a farthing a copy. They were also sent to family and friends all over England. In more recent times, the writer and Nobel Prize winner, William Golding, lived briefly in the vicarage during the Second World War. He loved the village so much that he returned to live for many years in Ebble Thatch along the Bowerchalke–Broadchalke road. His memorial stone can be seen in the graveyard.

Rev Edward Collett at work on his Parish Paper in Bowerchalke vicarage

3 Leave the churchyard by the front gate turning right (you will see the old National School, now the village hall, opposite the church). Carry on until you reach Costers Lane on the left. Turn here and follow it to the junction with another road. Turn right and almost immediately left on to a green track (SU 021 237). At the top of the incline this bears right and soon you will meet a junction of tracks (SU 019 245). (You may keep straight on here for a quicker

Rev Edward Collett outside Bowerchalke vicarage in the 1920s

return to Broadchalke). **Take the left track which climbs
over the downland and descends into Fifield Bavant.**

Note the church as you descend into the valley. It is one of the
smallest in the county and still in occasional use.

**4 Do *not* cross the river, but take the stile on the right.
This will take you onwards parallel with the Ebble River
through three gateways to reach the road (SU 024 249).**

This is known as 'Little London', and to your right lies a cottage
once owned by Sir Anthony Eden, Prime Minister of Great
Britain at the time of the Suez crisis, whose tomb lies further up
the valley in Alvediston Churchyard.

**5 Continue along the road until you see a footpath sign
on the left. Go through the kissing gate with care and
descend to a stile in front of you.**

**6 The path will take you over the river. Follow it right
and right again around a bungalow. This brings you to a
track (SU 027 251) which takes you left back to
Broadchalke parallel to the Ebble, with its watercress
beds on the right. Cross the road at Knapp Farm and veer
right through its garden along a grassy track past a
house. Carry on alongside the river until you emerge at a
road with a garage and petrol station opposite to the
right (SU 039 256). Turn right here. The road swings left
and you take the road opposite the *Queen's Head* back to
the car park.**

Bowerchalke church. The upper courses of the tower, which appear lighter than the lower stonework, were added during the Victorian restoration of the 1860.

Further Reading

Broad Chalke: A history of a South Wiltshire village, its land and people over 2000 Years by the People of the Village, 1999, (Baskerville Press)
Sawyer, R, 1989, *The Bowerchalke Parish Papers* (Alan Sutton)

14 History and Tranquillity

Dinton, Fovant and Compton Chamberlayne (6 miles/ 10 km)

by Rex and Sheila Sawyer   (OS Explorer 130, 143)

History abounds on this walk which takes in a National Trust village, two beautiful watermills, First World War hill carvings and a village with strong Civil War connections. Starting at the Wyndham Arms, *the second Dinton inn to bear that name, the walk proceeds through the village to the National Trust parkland of Philipps House and the picturesque Teffont Mill. Buzzards, partridges, hares and even deer are among the wild life to be seen, as one rises to the downland overlooking Fovant and the famous military badges carved from the chalk on the distant hillside. The walk passes near and through woodland on the way to Compton Chamberlayne, home of the Penruddocke family, one of whom resisted Cromwell's might and was beheaded for his rebellion. The walk concludes beyond a second tranquil watermill at Dinton. Parts of the valley can be very muddy after heavy rain.*

1 Start at the *Wyndham Arms* Car Park on the B3089 (SU 019 315). Turn right (as you face the road with the pub behind you), preferably crossing the road on to the pavement. After a few yards cross again into Spracklands.

There are masses of daffodils here in Spring. Further down the road towards Dinton village is the National Trust property of Little Clarendon, once the home of George Engleheart, a renowned horticulturalist who specialised in daffodils.

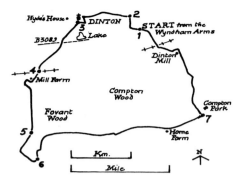

2 At the end of the road turn left into the small car park and through the kissing gate. Follow the path on the left of the field and on through two gates in a westerly direction. You will find another gate on the left into the next field. Carry on in the same direction to a gate next to a house. Follow the narrow path to the road (SU 009 317). Cross the road and proceed south then west around the church to the gate into the National Trust field.

The Church of St Mary's is worth a visit. It was described by Pevsner as 'a dignified church with the crossing tower at its centre, essentially Decorated, but with older and younger parts'.

Dinton fête day, *c.* 1904. The band and officials of the Wyndham Arms Slate Club, with their banner, lead the procession from St Mary's church after their service.

3 Cross the field diagonally, with the lake to your left, until you reach a stile (SU 006 313). Cross the busy road with care to the stile opposite and cross the field diagonally right to another stile. Continue on the same line over two further stiles into woodland (SU 003 309). A further stile will take you out of the woodland and then diagonally left across the field to the railway. Again, cross the railway *with care*.

As you cross the field you will see on the right the elegant Hyde's House and then Philipps House. Hyde House was once a rectory and the home of Edward Hyde, who was born in 1609 and christened in the church. A successful lawyer, he rose to become Lord Chancellor under Charles II. His daughter Anne married the future James II and was mother to both Queen Anne and Queen Mary. Philipps House was bought by the Wyndham family in 1689. In 1812 this wealthy landowning family employed Jeffry Wyatt (Sir Jeffry Wyatville) to remodel their home into the fashionable neo-classical mansion we see today. Bertram Philipps bought the estate in 1917 and renamed the property. In 1943 he gave the house and 203 acres of parkland to the National Trust. The grassland is now managed without fertilisers or sprays, thus regenerating the wildlife of the lake and the park.

4 **Proceed diagonally right to cross a little bridge just before Teffont Mill. Keep right around the paddock to a gate by the mill pond. Follow left around the millpond. Cross a stile and follow the River Nadder to the next stile on the right into a field. Cross the bridge in front of you. Go up the bank to the next stile. Cross the field and turn right along the fence. At the end of the field you will see a kissing gate slightly right of a field gate. Go through and diagonally left to the next kissing gate. Keep right around the brambles to next kissing gate. Cross the track into the next field and diagonally left to a field opening right of the woodland. Go through and follow the right hand side of the next field down to the end. Turn right over the stile.**

5 **Follow down the path and left through a rather boggy area by the stream to a further stile. Turn left and over the stile to cross the field to another stile. Turn left following the path to the road. Cross to a further stile and walk up the field to the woodland. Follow the wood round to the right and then left.**

This is a good point for a refreshment break. Find a comfortable spot on the downland and look around. Below, you can see Fovant nestling in the valley. Look ahead to the far downland and you can see examples of the famous Emblems on the hillside. Nine of these were originally constructed in 1916 by troops training at Fovant Camp, one of the largest training and transit camps established to train the 'New Army'. They are the largest group of hillside figures in Europe. Alternatively, if you are making this a day walk, you can get a meal at the *Pembroke Arms*. Simply cross the next stile, turn right and follow the track to the A30. The pub is to your right.

An aerial view of the Fovant badges below the Iron Age hillfort of Chiselbury Camp. Behind can be seen the line of the old Salisbury to Shaftesbury road, a main road to the west before the A30 was developed from 1792.

Compton Chamberlayne House. Built originally in Tudor Gothic style in 1550 by Sir Edward Penruddocke, it was later remodelled in the early Stuart style and remained with the family until 1930.

6 After your break, cross the stile and turn left along the edge of the wood. Cross the next stile and continue on with the woods to your left and the Emblems to the right. The next stile on the left takes you down on to a track.

COMPTON CHAMBERLAYNE This tiny village, with its single street lined with a rich variety of local-stone cottages, displays with pride its 'Best Kept Small Village In Wiltshire' sign won on a number of occasions. A brief reference in the Domesday Book indicates that its earlier name was *Contone*, meaning a village in the valley. In the church, which you can visit through a gate in the wall of the mansion, you will see that the chancel floor is raised. This was to accommodate the many tombs of the Penruddocke family who built the adjoining Compton House, originally in Tudor Gothic, in 1550. They were to reside there for almost four centuries. Most notable among the family was Sir John Penruddocke, who had lost a brother in the Civil War but continued to press for the restoration of Charles II to the throne. On 12 March 1655, accompanied by other prominent Royalist leaders, he marched into Salisbury with 200 men, but was unenthusiastically received. The company then galloped westwards hoping to reach further allies in Cornwall with an army of men recruited on the way. It was not to be. At South Molton they were intercepted by Cromwell's regimental cavalry stationed at Exeter. After a pitched battle, many of the Royalists fled. The remainder, including John Penruddocke, were taken as prisoners to Exeter where, with his co-conspirators, he was beheaded.

Turn left here and almost immediately right into the woodland. After about a half-mile (0.8km), the path runs out right into a field. Turn left and continue on easterly for about a mile (1.6km) until descending into Compton Chamberlayne.

7 From the track turn left on to the road and follow it out of the village. Where the road bends to the right, take the track on the left to Dinton Mill. Turn left around the mill and follow the track back, across the railway, to the busy road. To the left you will see your starting point, the *Wyndham Arms*.

Further Reading

Sawyer, R, 1995, *Tales of a Wiltshire Valley* (Alan Sutton)
Church Guide, 2000, *Dinton, A brief Guide to St Mary's Church* (Mark Allen)

15 A Wander to Wardour

Tisbury, Hatch and Wardour

(5.5 miles / 8.8km)

by Ken Watts   (OS Explorer 118)

This walk follows an indirect circular route from Tisbury through Hatch to Wardour and back to Tisbury. Its particular associations are literary, architectural and historical. Tisbury lies 12 miles (19.2km) west of Salisbury and 7 miles (11.2km) north-east of Shaftesbury, and has public toilets, car parking, shops and public houses. The Tisbury district is associated with three 20th-century writers – Rudyard Kipling, Arthur Ransome and Edward Thomas. The walk passes the largest Georgian country house in Wiltshire, and after crossing a former medieval deer park also passes a castle which sustained two sieges in the Civil War. Old Wardour Castle is now administered by English Heritage and is open to the public. The walk is over broken country of downland and woods described by Ransome as 'very good walking country' at the head of the Nadder Valley. The terrain undulates but there are no really steep hills. Part of the walk is on very minor winding roads but it is emphasised that no places offering refreshments are passed on the walk and so necessary refreshments must be carried.

1 The walk starts from Tisbury parish church of St John the Baptist at ST 944 292 in Church Street at the lower end of Tisbury west of The Square. There are public car parks nearby. Commence the walk by turning your back on the church and walking north up the narrow alley marked

with a yellow arrow, which runs between walls from Church Street directly opposite the church. After continuing straight up this path for about 200m, at a minor road turn left (west) and walk along this road out of Tisbury. Where the road forks ignore the right fork, which is an uphill ramp, take the left fork and follow the road downhill and on west through Tuckingmill. A short distance beyond a road junction with a public telephone box on your left diverge left from the road by walking south-west down a lane lined with quarry houses. Continue straight on through a gate south-west across open fields. About 600m after leaving the road at the edge of a dry coombe pass through a pedestrian gate on your right, then continue straight on down a fence line into the coombe, but incline slightly right to pass right of a pond in the coombe bottom and follow the right side of a hedgeline up the opposite slope. Continue straight on to pass immediately right of the modern outbuildings and barns of East Hatch Farm and enter the minor road at East Hatch (2) at ST 926 285. Across the road at a road junction to the left is the farmhouse.

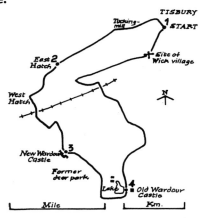

Hatch in a place-name generally means 'gate into a wood or forest'. East Hatch Farm was for some years from 1911 rented by the writer Arthur Ransome (1884–1967), who in 1913 left his wife Ivy and daughter Tabitha at Hatch and went to Russia as a newspaper correspondent. He described East Hatch Farm as: 'a two-storeyed grey house with mullioned windows', and describes how:

> It stood on a narrow lane that ran through the hamlet about a quarter of a mile above the little River Nadder. . . From the garden there was an open view across the valley to the woods of Wardour and the high ridge of the Downs. It was in very good walking

RUDYARD KIPLING AND TISBURY While visiting Tisbury walkers may be interested in the fact that Rudyard Kipling (1865–1936) was often at Tisbury from 1894 until 1911 after his parents retired there from India. Their son Rudyard and his wife Carrie in 1894 rented Arundell House on the east side of the top of Tisbury High Street to be near his parents. Kipling joined Tisbury cricket club and took an active interest in the local history of Tisbury. He and his wife were at Tisbury in 1900–1 at about the time that *Kim* was published. Kipling's father, John Lockwood Kipling (1837–1911), was a Yorkshire-born artist and craftsman in the Arts and Crafts style of William Morris. He had gone to India in 1865 as Professor of Architectural Sculpture at Bombay University and became principal of Lahore School of Art (1875–93). He remained in India for almost thirty years and advised Queen Victoria on the Indian style of the Durbar Hall at Osborne House on the Isle of Wight. Rudyard was born at Bombay and was particularly close to his father, who became both his literary adviser and the illustrator of some of his books, including *The Jungle Books* (1894–5) which were part written by Rudyard at Tisbury. When he retired to Tisbury he and his wife Alice lived at Diane Lodge in Hindon Lane (which they renamed The Gables), situated at the north end of Tisbury. Rudyard Kipling took the drafts of *The Jungle Books* and *Puck of Pook's Hill* (1906) to Tisbury to be discussed with his father, who was always his most trusted critic. During 1900 he was often at Tisbury to consult his father about *Kim* (1901), for which Lockwood Kipling provided the illustrations using a local schoolboy as the model for *Kim*, and local tradesmen for the other characters. Kipling's mother Alice (1837–1910) was the eldest of four daughters of a methodist minister called Macdonald. All four sisters became interested in art and were published writers. Georgiana married the painter Burne-Jones, Agnes married another painter Edward Poynter, Louise painted with both Burne-Jones and William Morris but married an iron-founder, and Alice married Lockwood Kipling. In November 1910, having aged rapidly due to the stress she suffered in caring for her beautiful disturbed married daughter 'Trix', Alice Kipling died and was buried at Tisbury. Within two months of her death her husband Lockwood also died, when visiting the Wyndhams at Clouds at East Knoyle, and was buried in an adjoining grave. Their graves are marked by two large slabs near the south-east corner of the church.

country within easy reach of Salisbury and Hazlitt's Winterslow and to the west Shaftesbury.

Ransome's friend the poet Edward Thomas (1878-1917) (who had helped to find him East Hatch Farm) came here in early 1917 from embarkation camp at Codford for a last visit to his 'daughter the younger' Myfanwy, then aged six, who was staying with Ivy Ransome and Tabitha. His diary reads:

27 January 1917: Letter to say Baba [Myfanwy] was at Ransome's, so I walked over the Downs by Chicklade Bottom and the Fonthills to Hatch, and blistered both feet badly. House full of ice and big fires [1917 was an exceptionally harsh winter]. Sat up with Ivy till 12 and slept till 8. Another fine frosty day on the 28th . . . Rested my feet, talking to the children or Ivy cooking with Kitty Gurd [the maid]. Hired a bicycle to save walking. Such a beautiful ride after joining the Mere and Amesbury road at Fonthill Bishop [on his way back to Codford].

The following morning Edward Thomas embarked for France where he was killed in April 1917.

2 From East Hatch Farm continue south-west down Ransome's 'narrow lane' that winds through East Hatch, ignoring the road on your left. Follow the lane left as it turns south at West Hatch and immediately after crossing a bridge over the railway leave the lane by a stile on the left (at ST 923 276) and follow the public footpath south-west across a field. Cross the tiny River Nadder by the footbridge and join the Semley to Tisbury road at ST 925 274 opposite the school. Walk left (north-east) along the road for about 200m and at the first road junction (ST 926 275) turn right (south) up the road towards New Wardour Castle. After about 300m, where the road bends left (ST 927 273) leave the road by continuing straight ahead and follow the footpath past the entrance front of New Wardour Castle.

The name Wardour is believed to derive from two Old English words, *weard* meaning watch and *ora* meaning slope. New Wardour Castle is a huge and rather bleak Palladian house, the largest Georgian house in Wiltshire, built in 1769–76 to the design of James Paine for the Arundell family. It is designed in the typical Palladian tripartite arrangement, with a large pedimented central block and smaller flanking wings. As catholics the Arundells were allowed a chapel only on condition that it was concealed within the fabric of the house – the chapel is embedded in one of the wings. Pevsner described New Wardour Castle as 'stern', but considered its circular staircase hall to be 'the most glorious Georgian interior of Wiltshire'. Having been for long a school the house is now divided into flats and is not accessible.

New Wardour Castle, built in 1769–76 by the Arundells to replace Old Wardour Castle

3 After passing in front of New Wardour Castle swing left (east) for a few metres and then turn right through a gate and follow the field footpath south-east across fields that were formerly the deer park to Old Wardour Castle. Pass west of Ark Farm from ST 934 266, following the loop of track which runs first south and then east and north to Old Wardour Castle. The latter part of this track was formerly the main drive to the castle.

Old Wardour Castle is now administered by English Heritage and is open to the public. It was first crenellated in 1393 and over the years was developed into a fortified hexagonal tower house standing in a bailey (outer courtyard) surrounded by a curtain wall, all now rather battered after sustaining two sieges in the Civil War. Later additions to the castle include a grotto on a terrace within the bailey on the east side, a Georgian gothick pavilion built on to the west bailey wall, and a house built against the bailey wall on the south side of the castle. The former deer parks were landscaped in the 18th century when the lake was formed. Wardour was an ancient estate and perhaps a royal one, as there is a reference to King Alfred in the 9th

PALLADIANISM At the time when prestigious buildings in England were being built in a fundamentally Tudor style with classical elements arbitrarily grafted on, Andrea Palladio (1508–80) – often described as the most imitated architect in history – initiated in Italy a severely classical style of building based on strict classical prcedent and proportion, as a reaction against the current exuberant Mediterranean baroque style. The Palladian style was introduced into England by Inigo Jones (1573–1652), although after his death it was transformed into the restrained English baroque style practised by Sir Christopher Wren (1632–1723). In 1715 the new royal house of Hanover, wanting a change in architectural style to mark its accession, revived the Palladian style, which became for most of the 18th century almost universally used for important buildings.

century giving a judgement on a dispute, 'while he stood washing his hands within the chamber there'.

Being strongly catholic the Arundells sided with Charles I in the Civil War, but when Sir Thomas Hungerford and the Wiltshire republican Edmund Ludlow appeared before Wardour the Arundell fighting men were away and the castle was held by the doughty Blanche, Lady Arundell (1583–1649), then aged sixty, a grand-daughter of Margaret Countess of Salisbury and the second wife of the 1st Baron Arundell. In her husband's absence Lady Blanche heroically defended Wardour Castle with only about twenty-five fighting men, courageously holding out for five days until the castle was undermined and partially blown up and she was forced to surrender. The articles of the surrender were then broken. The ladies were given safe conduct and were sent to Shaftesbury, but they were deprived of all their possessions and left with only the clothes that they were wearing. The castle was also looted and five cartloads of plunder were sent off to Shaftesbury. It was wryly suggested by the royalists that: 'The one use of the inventory was to let the world know what my Lord Arundell lost and what these rebels gained'.

After Hungerford departed leaving Ludlow as the parliamentary governor of Wardour young Henry 2nd Lord Arundell, whose father had died at the royalist headquarters at Oxford, arrived before Wardour with some cavalry and demanded its surrender, although his unsupported cavalry posed no threat to the castle. In December 1643 Captain Christopher Bowyer appeared at Wardour with infantry and the castle was closely invested but Ludlow stubbornly resisted. After Captain Bowyer was killed he was succeeded by Colonel Barnes, who erected a siege work on the hill and continued to invest the castle without assaulting it. As Ludlow's garrison began to run short of provisions the royalist commander summoned reinforcements under Sir Francis Dodington, and he brought up some Irish troops who took an active part in the final stages of the siege. Dodington invited Ludlow to surrender but he stoutly held out until 16 March when he agreed to negotiate. On 18 March he met Dodington and Arundell in the grounds and grudgingly surrendered the castle after having resisted for three months. According to his *Memoirs* he surrendered against his will and only because his men had become discouraged. Ludlow's sick and wounded were held at Wardour for a time before being sent to Bristol.

Ruins of Old Wardour Castle with its 18th-century Gothick pavilion left

4 From Old Wardour Castle continue north passing immediately left (west) of the castle car park along the track through woods (not marked on the definitive maps as a public right-of-way but accepted by Wiltshire County Council as such) and at a road junction (ST 939 270) follow the minor road which runs for about three-quarters of a mile (1.2km) first north-east and then north-west to Hazeldon (ST 934 279). There cross the road, walk a short distance right (north-east), and then take the minor road left (north-west). Carefully cross the railway crossing and, after continuing for about 350 metres west, at a road junction ignore the road joining from the south-west, turn right and walk a very short distance north-west and cross

the stile high on your right (ST 929 283) and follow the
footpath which runs a little north of east across fields
above the River Nadder past Wick Wood Farm. At Wick Farm
(ST 941 286), on the site of the deserted village of Wick,
swing left (north-east) and after a short distance turn right
and follow the footpath north-east back to the start point
of the walk at Tisbury Church.

Further Reading

Watts, Ken, 1998, *Exploring Historic Wiltshire: volume 2, South*,
   chapter 11 (Ex Libris Press)

16 Five Counties and 150 Million Years

Win Green and Berwick St John

(5.5 miles / 8.5 km; can be extended to 7.5 miles / 12 km)

by Isobel Geddes   (OS Explorer 118)

This walk starts and finishes at Win Green on the ancient trackway, known as the Ox Drove, running along the top of the Chalk escarpment at the northern edge of Cranborne Chase. The magnificent panorama needs a clear day, when it extends northwards across Wiltshire as far as the Marlborough Downs, westwards into Dorset's Blackmore Vale and south to the coastal Purbeck Hills. Berwick St John provides a contrast to the Chalk downland, as it nestles one hundred and fifty metres below in the shadow of Winkelbury, an Iron Age hill-fort. A track runs down the side of this once-fortified spur to a lane leading to the village; the route returns to Win Green up another downland track with an easy gradient. To enjoy the fine views further, the walk can be extended by 2 miles (3.5km), following the ridge top for another mile before descending over Trow Down to a lane in the valley a mile or so east of Berwick St John. Built of the Greensand on which it rests, the village has a fine pub. Mud can be a problem in places after wet weather.

1 **Starting from the parking area on Win Green (ST 923 205), walk towards the clump of trees, stopping to look at the plinth near the triangulation pillar.**

The circular plaque on top of the plinth indicates the various landmarks visible in all directions. At 277 metres (911 feet), it

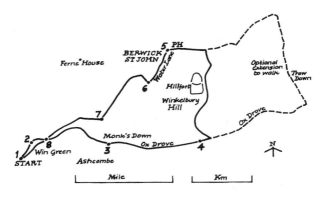

is at the summit of Cranborne Chase, so the dramatic panorama
stretches all the way to the Needles on the Isle of Wight, only
32 miles (51km.) to the south-east; the Purbeck Hills mark the
Dorset coast to the south, while the Blackmore Vale lies to the
west. The Mendips form the north-western horizon and
Salisbury Plain is to the north-east. Remarkably, beyond
Salisbury Plain, Milk Hill and Tan Hill can be seen on a clear
day; they are the the the highest hills of Wiltshire (294m./964ft.).
This is a good point to give a thought to the layers of rock
underlying this landscape. The Chalk, several hundred metres of
fine white limestone, lies at the top of the pile; you are
standing on it. Beneath is a sandstone, known as the Upper
Greensand, because of its greenish-grey colour. It is around 70
metres thick. The plateau-like hills it forms are frequently
wooded and, like the Chalk above, have steep scarp edges.
Donhead Clift is one of these; it can be seen above Donhead
St.Mary in the valley of the infant Nadder. The river rises in
these permeable sandstone hills; the water can sink no lower as
there are clays below – so springs appear.

All these rocks are Cretaceous in age, laid down in the sea
between 75 and 110 million years ago. Below again are Jurassic
rocks, limestones above, clay underneath, representing the
deposits of 150 million year-old seas. So imagine this whole
area below the sea for as long as it has been hill country – and
tropical seas at that, at a time before Europe had drifted north
to present latitudes. The river systems have cut through these
layers to reveal the oldest rocks at the bottom of their valleys:
down in the Blackmore Vale the River Stour has taken
advantage of soft Jurassic clays, creating a broad plain, while
the Jurassic limestone rocks are exposed along the course of
the Nadder in the Vale of Wardour, providing the famous pale
building stones, much-used locally, including for Salisbury
Cathedral.

Cranborne Chase, once a medieval hunting ground, was a private chase belonging to the Duke of Gloucester – until King John married the duke's daughter, Isabella, when it passed to the king. The woodland was formerly more extensive, reaching as far north as the River Nadder; hunting rights were maintained until 1828.

CHALK (magnified 5000 times) This rock, a soft white limestone, was laid down in warm seas around 75-100 million years ago, building up to a thickness of over 300 metres. It is made up of the microscopic remains of planktonic one-celled algae known as coccoliths; such algae are still around today. They secrete simple calcite plates, one hundredth of a millimetre across, which overlap to form coccolith rings supporting the algal cells. The algae were the main food of shrimp-like creatures called copepods and it is thought that for the plates from dead algae to be heavy enough to sink and accumulate as an ooze on the sea floor, they had to be eaten and passed through these copepods. Fossil remains of other marine life can be found within the chalk; the flints are derived from sponges which have silica skeletons.

2 Heading around the left side of the clump of beeches, you will find a footpath below the trees running into the Ox Drove track; here turn right.

The impressive views are now over the Vale of Wardour. This follows a line of geological weakness, an upfold where the rocks have been stretched along the top of the fold, making them more susceptible to erosion. The River Nadder follows this line, where the Jurassic limestones appear at the surface along the centre of its valley. They are hard to discern, but are flanked to north and south by the tree-covered Upper Greensand hills. Above again is the Chalk which rises to the northern and eastern horizons. You will notice an extra tongue of Chalk downland, the back of White Sheet Hill north of Berwick St John. Its presence is due to another upfold, the axis of which runs from the east into the Vale of Wardour here, resulting in the smaller parallel valley, opening out westwards at Berwick St John and continuing eastwards, where the weakness is picked out by the River Ebble.

As you follow the track, Ashcombe descends steeply to the south, appropriately wooded with ash trees. There is a footpath leading south towards Tollard Royal, another lovely walk, especially in autumn when the leaves are turning. It has a good pub and the charming Larmer Tree Gardens. But save that for another day – the geology is more interesting on this route! Berwick St John has an even better pub.

Down below, to the north is Ferne House, now rebuilt. The estate once provided employment for the villagers and the daughter of the house was for a time engaged to the poet Shelley, her cousin. A short distance east of Ferne is Berwick St John, below and to the left of Winkelbury Hill.

3 **The track reaches a crossing of the ways (ST 937 207) at the surfaced lane coming up the escarpment; go straight ahead down on to this lane (the track veers off to the right) and continue eastward.**

Despite the tarmac, this is still the Ox Drove, following the ridge. There are Scots pines on the right, on either edge of the wood, marking the route, a tree traditionally planted along such ancient tracks. If you have an aversion to tarmac there is a little footpath running through the wood, parallel to the road, which affords views over the ridge to the south, at least until the trees come into leaf.

4 **After the turn-off down to Berwick St.John and past the 'No Through Road' sign, carry straight on, on to the track (which can be muddy) signposted 'By-way to Ox Drove' and enter the strip of woodland (leaving the surfaced road at a bend to the south-east, ST 952 207). If the Ox Drove proves too muddy, or you want a shorter route to Berwick St John, this is the point where a decision must be made; to carry on along the ridge top extends the walk by a further 2 miles (3km.). After 200m, there is a track branching off to**

The Ox Drove above Berwick St John

the left (ST 954 208). If you take this shorter option, turn sharply left and head out on to the open downland of Winkelbury Hill. This track dwindles to a footpath as it descends the spur into a hollow way. After merging with another track, it hits the lane just east of Berwick St John (ST 954 223). Turn left into the village – it is only 650 metres to the centre and the pub, the *Talbot Inn*. For the longer option, carry on along the Ox Drove; when you leave the trees, it is one mile (1.7 km.) along the ridge until a well-defined track off to the left (ST 970 213). Turn left here (northwards) over Trow Down until you reach the lane in the valley bottom (ST 966 229). Go left down this road to Berwick St John, a mile and a quarter distant (2km.)

THE OX DROVE This ridgeway follows the Chalk escarpment along the northern edge of Cranborne Chase. From the late Middle Ages until the mid 19th century, cattle and sheep drovers used it to drive their animals from Dorset and Somerset to the towns, London in particular, as they expanded and needed food from further afield. The coming of the railways and cattle-trucks made it redundant. Even before that time, the route's importance was reduced when the Ebble valley road opened in the mid-18th century, leaving this track solely to the drovers.

The short cut down the side of Winkelbury Hill takes you through a hollow way lined with wood garlic and sprinkled with primroses in spring.

On the longer route, after leaving the woodland, still with the line of Scots pine at its edge, further downland views present themselves. There may be deer bounding down the hillside and skylarks soaring above. The characteristic in-flight warbling of these birds has the dual purpose of attracting a mate and demarcating territory, so is most noticeable in spring; they remain practically silent in August and September. To the north are the two Chalk ridges separated by the Vale of Wardour; immediatedly ahead to the left is Windmill Hill just beyond the lane below. This marks the watershed, within the valley, where the River Ebble rises (just west of the hill) and flows eastwards to join with the River Avon south of Salisbury. To the right are fine views over the woods and fields of Cranborne Chase, reaching southwards into Dorset. As you turn northward over Trow Down, superb views to the west down the valley to Berwick St John appear. A patchwork of fields is framed by the hills of Winkelbury to the south and White Sheet to the north. The track's banks expose some of the underlying Chalk, a reminder that all this was once under a tropical sea.

> WINKELBURY This is a typical Iron Age promontory hill-fort, occupied by Celtic people in the first century B.C. It began with simple ramparts across the top of the spur, defending the access to the promontory. Subsequently ramparts were added at the sides around the top of the promontory and additional inner ramparts were built across between the side banks. A later, Anglo-Saxon cemetery has also been discovered on Winkelbury Hill.

As you walk back along the lane, notice the tree-lined Ox Drove up on the ridge-top to the south. The earthworks of Winkelbury can be discerned ahead, then Win Green's distinctive beech clump appears beyond, marking the location of the car! The lane goes from the Chalk to the Upper Greensand below and becomes more sunken, as the sands are so soft that they eroded easily under the wheels of carts over hundreds of years. As you pass the turn-off to Cross Farm on the right, you can see the bed-rock on the corner: a greenish-grey sandstone with dark green speckles of the iron mineral which gives the sand its greenish colour. It is riddled with insect holes. There is plenty of this sandstone to be seen in the houses of Berwick St John, including the pub. Perhaps it is time for a stop there! – a charming traditional establishment with excellent food too.

5 The *Talbot Inn* is open from 12.00-2.30pm and 12.00-4.00pm on Sundays (lunch has to be ordered by 2.15); it opens in the evening at 6.30pm. From the *Talbot Inn*, cross the road and turn left into Water Lane by the quaint bus-shelter, going around the corner past the entrance to Easton Farm and along the lane.

Greensand buildings, Berwick St John

Water Lane is aptly named. It has a stream running alongside it which does not always keep to its bed. The Upper Greensand is water-bearing, like the Chalk, and as it is underlain by clay, which prevents further downward movement of the water, springs commonly emerge from it. There are some nice Greensand cottages on the right. Winkelbury stands up behind the houses to the left.

6 Turn right up the side lane before the bend (ST 944 218) and then, shortly after, turn left at the farm up a track signposted 'Bridleway'.

Winkelbury dominates the view to the east as you round the bend; the banks of the fortification can be clearly seen. Ahead, up on the sky-line, is the return destination – Win Green, topped by its round clump of beeches.

7 The main track continues to the left of the wood ahead. Fork right up the track which enters the wood (ST 936

212), then right again shortly after to reduce the steepness of the climb and avoid retracing the outward route as much as possible; (this track is not marked on the Ordnance Survey map). This brings you out at a stile on to the road opposite another track (ST 933 212). Follow the latter over a stile a short way up and diagonally up the hill.

Look back across the Vale of Wardour to the Upper Greensand hills; the nearest are Donhead Clift and Barkers Hill. Their bedrock dips southwards beneath the Chalk on which you stand. Beyond, on the far side of the vale are Beacon Hill and Fonthill, again covered in trees, well-suited to their sandy soils. Behind Ferne House, the Chalk of Whitesheet Hill rises up, and to its left the wooded Greensands again dip beneath. The Chalk scarp here is stepped by terracettes. Often called sheep-tracks, they are actually the result of downhill soil-creep over the millennia.

8 There is a stile/gate at the junction with the Ox Drove. Cross this track and take the path past the National Trust sign heading for the beech trees of Win Green ahead. Keep left of the trees, then the car park is directly beyond the triangulation point.

To the left, Ashcombe appears again below, and beyond are other woods and downs of Cranborne Chase. As you rise the view widens until once again Wiltshire, Dorset, Somerset, Hampshire and the Isle of Wight too are spread before you in all directions.

Further Reading

Geddes, I. 2000, *Hidden Depths: Wiltshire's Geology & Landscapes*. (Ex Libris Press, Bradford-on -Avon).
Watts, K. 1998, *Exploring Historic Wiltshire: volume 2: South*. (Ex Libris Press, Bradford-on-Avon).

17 Lily's Walk

East Knoyle and Milton (2.7 miles / 4.4 km)

by John Chandler   (OS Explorer 143)

I asked contributors to this book to select their favourite walks in south Wiltshire, and they have come up with the most memorable and spectacular from their wide experience of walking in the area. My favourite walk is rather different, in that it became part of my daily life for many years. Accompanied by Lily (a German Shepherd crossed – so far as we could tell – with a much smaller terrier, which gave her the appearance of a fox) I undertook almost daily this walk, or variations on it, in rain or shine, until old age rendered it beyond her capability. For me this is God's own walk: woods, attractive lanes and cottages, a stunning view, plenty of history – and a pub for sitting outside with the dog halfway round. Especially on a summer evening, it is the perfect relaxation after a busy day.

The walk uses minor, occasionally steep, public roads for much of its course, although there are field paths on the return leg, which can be wet and muddy after inclement weather. At various places you may encounter alpaca, which graze in many of the local fields. East Knoyle is an attractive, friendly village, and in addition to the pub visited in the course of this walk (the Fox and Hounds*), there is another excellent establishment, the* Seymour Arms, *close to the walk's starting/ finishing point in the village.*

1 **Park near the War Memorial in the centre of East Knoyle village (ST 881 305). You could walk up to the church (3) straight away, but a few minutes spent exploring the village street by a short detour will be well rewarded.**

Until 1996 the road which bends around the terraced garden and children's play area was part of the main A350 route from west

Wiltshire into Dorset, and walking along the village street was not recommended. Now by-passed, East Knoyle is a quiet and pleasant place to live and work. The public garden, Knoyle House Grounds, was the terraced garden surrounding a country mansion of the Seymour family, Knoyle House, which was demolished in 1960 for road widening. The plaque near its entrance commemorates Sir Christopher Wren, whose birthplace was a cottage, long vanished (and towards the end of its life known as Haslam's Shop), which stood on the corner of Wise Lane opposite the present post office.

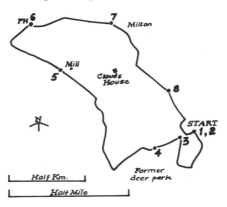

2 Walk southwards (Knoyle House Grounds to your left) along the street, passing an archway into the former grounds and then Millbrook Lane on your left, and note the pleasant mixture of cottages and larger village houses, some using blocks of the local Greensand as building material. Opposite the petrol garage notice the former Congregational chapel, with its manse and Sunday school (Jupe's School, from where, incidentally, this book was published). Take the path to the right past Jupe's School, which immediately forks left and gives access through a gate to a field. Follow the tarmac path across this field and then, bearing right, through three more gates to rejoin Church Road by St Mary's Church.

These fields, and the private woods to their left, form one end of a large medieval hunting park, which was enclosed by a park pale and extended about 1km southward, behind all the houses along the village street. East Knoyle belonged to the bishops of Winchester who, in the early medieval period, were among the wealthiest and most influential men in England. Like royalty and nobility they enjoyed venison on their table, and so maintained their own parks to ensure its supply. The park pale can still be traced, and I have often seen deer frequenting the field and woods. I suspect that, until the park was created (it is first recorded in 1253) cottages and gardens existed in the area of our path, and that the earthworks in these fields are their remains.

St Mary's church preserves hints of its Saxon origins. If you walk round outside to inspect the north wall of the chancel you can just make out blind arcading rather like that at Bradford on Avon's Saxon chapel, and the north door looks distinctly Saxon. Inside there are monuments to members of the Seymour and Wyndham families, and spectacular plasterwork panels in the chancel showing Biblical scenes. These were designed by Christopher Wren's father and made in about 1639.

3 **After exploring the church walk slowly along Church Road westwards, noticing the medieval arched window and doorway of the village hall, the unusual cottage on the left and the ornate former school on the right, until you arrive at a driveway and a lane entering from the right.**

Until 1856 Church Road was a cul de sac, and ended in a farmyard more or less opposite the village hall. The windowless cottage on the left survives from this farmyard, as do the footings of a large barn (burnt down in 1961). The smaller portion of the village hall has a medieval doorway and is believed to be part of the farmhouse belonging to the bishop of Winchester's estate. After the road was opened up a new village school was built (in 1872-3); its remarkable near-eastern Muslim style windows (by G H Aitchison) add an exotic touch to the village architecture. What would Wren have made of them? Knoyle Place, the house approached through the gate piers, is the former rectory, and the older surviving portion (left as viewed from the road) would have been the home of Wren senior and his family.

4 **Keeping Knoyle Place on your right continue up the lane, past the entrance to the village cemetery, and round a dark bend. (At the far side of the cemetery there is an interesting enclosure containing monuments to members of the Wyndham family, designed by Detmar Blow) The lane climbs and then levels into Holloway, where it is lined with attractive cottages. Continue to the end of the lane and, at the junction with Holloway Lane, bear sharp right, pausing at the field gate to admire the view**

Knoyle Place

(ST 876 303). The lane continues with good views to the left and then, as it climbs up on to the Greensand, it finds itself in a deep cutting. At the end of the cutting turn right, up a steep and twisting tarmac lane in woodland (always to me more reminiscent of Sussex than Wiltshire!) until at the top you arrive at a T junction (ST 875 308). Turn left and after about 150m carry straight across the road junction (signed The Green and Upton). The woodland peters out and you find a large area of open common land, with (by the seats) a breathtaking view to the left, and the tower of a windmill looking down on you from the right.

The name 'Knoyle' is supposed to derive from an early form of the word 'knuckle', referring to the bumpy knuckle-like appearance of this Greensand ridge, which forms the village's backcloth. Having no reliable water-power (the parish straddles the Nadder and Stour watershed) we seem not to have been very successful with watermills. Windmills are a medieval invention, and one is recorded at Knoyle in the 14th century. The surviving tower may be that of the mill recorded as new in 1536. After it ceased working in the Victorian period it was retained as a feature by the Clouds estate, although its sails and original cap (recorded on old photographs) have gone. It was repaired in about 1911 as a kind of belvedere.

The view scans the claylands of Blackmore Vale and is closed, on a clear day, by the chalk hills of mid-Dorset, between Dorchester and Sturminster Newton. The prominent rounded hill standing up from the vale is Duncliffe, between Shaftesbury and East Stour. Shaftesbury itself is perched on the hill to the left, beyond the wooded Kingsettle Hill. To the right the high ground is the wooded ridge of Selwood Forest, ending at Penselwood beyond Mere. The foreground sweeps away to a network of enclosed pasture fields, which have replaced the medieval park of Mere and the royal forest of Gillingham. The busy town of Gillingham itself can best be located as night falls, when its streetlights locate it. Beyond them the lights in the far distance belong to Stalbridge, another small Dorset town.

5 By the seats veer left slightly from the tarmac road, and walk to the left of the trees. You will see a path straight ahead of you where the open ground ends and the scrubby

---

SIR CHRISTOPHER WREN East Knoyle's most famous son, Wren was born here on 20 October 1632. He was the son of the rector and, but for a fire which entailed its renovation, he would have been born in what is now the older portion of Knoyle Place, then the rectory. In fact he was born in a cottage in the village. Wren's father, also Christopher, was an eminent and well-connected churchman who went on to become Dean of Windsor in 1636, and so took the infant genius with him and away from the village. Sir Christopher's connection with his birthplace is, therefore, quite slight, although he continued to hold land in the parish until 1662.

A prodigious child, Wren studied at Oxford and was appointed professor of astronomy, first in London (1657), then at Oxford (1661). He was a founder member of the Royal Society at this time, and designed the Sheldonian Theatre in Oxford. After the great fire of 1666 he was appointed to the commission for rebuilding London, and in 1669 as surveyor general to the crown. He embarked on the design of the city churches, and in particular St Paul's Cathedral for which he is best remembered. He also built for successive monarchs grand buildings of state, including Kensington Palace and Chelsea Hospital. St Paul's was completed in 1708, but Wren continued as surveyor general until 1718, well into his eighties.

He died in 1723, having created a new style of architecture, and through collaborating with them over many years, schooled up his successors, Hawksmoor and Vanbrugh to develop his style well into the eighteenth century. As a biographer has said of him, he was to architecture what Shakespeare was to literature.

woodland begins. Take this and, when after 250m you encounter another footpath climbing up through the woods from the left, join it as it bends towards the right (ST 870 312). Do not take the path to the right which leads up to bungalows, but continue more or less straight on the route which takes you behind their back gardens. The path opens out, and across the Green is a pub, the *Fox and Hounds*.

The view here from the Green looks westward and is less panoramic than the southward prospect from the windmill. The woodland behind Stourhead can be located by the presence of Alfred's Tower, and to its left sits the town of Mere; at dusk you can make out the lights of traffic on the main road, the A303, in the distance.

6 From the pub walk down to the lower end of the Green and take the lane on the left, before the telephone box (ST 871 313). After 200m look for a stile on the right (opposite Moorlands Cottage) which takes you into a field. The footpath crosses the field diagonally, and once over the brow you should head for the gap between bushes, through which a house with three large double chimneys can be seen. Continue down to the gate and stile in front of this house.

Milton lies equidistant between the two other settlements in the parish (Upton and East Knoyle), and its name, which means 'middle settlement' reflects this. Approaching it across the fields it seems the quintessence of the English countryside – handsome cottages, a few larger, rambling houses, a peaceful lane, a backdrop of woods and fields.

7 Turn right on to the lane and walk down through Milton. At the lowest point, where the lane bends left between houses and former farm buildings, climb the steep narrow footpath (partly stepped) to the right, emerging beside Hill Cottage. Cross the lane and continue on the footpath, which brings you to a drive in front of an ornate brick house. Do not turn left past the front of this house, but continue in a more-or-less straight line along the side of the house until you reach a kissing gate (ST 878 310). Through this you enter Clouds Park. There are two paths leading away from this gate. You should take the more southerly, which leads you away from the house down towards the lowest part of the park. Leave the park by the gate and stile at the bottom.

Clouds, named after a Tudor owner, existed as a small estate in Milton long before the present house was built in 1881-3, and there had been successive earlier houses on the same site. What one encounters today is the result of the purchase in 1877 by Percy Wyndham of part of the Seymours' East Knoyle estate, and his decision to build here 'the house of the age'. It is a remarkable house. It was designed by the Arts and Crafts architect Philip Webb for a couple (Percy and his wife Madeline) with sophisticated tastes, daring morals and a profound social conscience. It became the venue for innumerable glittering house parties in the late Victorian and Edwardian years – an embodiment of the world of Henry James, who was one of the guests. The family, and the house, never recovered from a series of deaths, father, son and grandson, in 1911, 1913 and 1914. It declined, became an anachronism and was sold in 1936. After a career as a nursery for unwanted babies it has been since 1983 a treatment centre for drug and alcohol dependency.

8 At the gate turn right, and you will find that the track soon becomes tarmac as it climbs, past a large house (Slades) on the right, to a road junction. Turn right (taking care on the blind corners) up the steep hill for 50m then, where the lanes divide, take the left fork. Shortly you will see steps leading down to a path which runs along the eastern side of the churchyard. This will take you back to Church Road and the war memorial, where the walk began. If you should feel the need for (further) refreshment by now drive down the village street (in the southerly direction you first walked), and after some 500m you will find the *Seymour Arms* on your left.

Further Reading

Claydon, Anthony, 2002
    (forthcoming), *The Nature of
    Knoyle* (Hobnob Press)
Dakers, Caroline, 1993, *Clouds: the
    biography of a country house*
    (Yale UP)
Victoria History of Wiltshire, vol. 11,
    1980, pp. 82-98

Lily

The Contributors

John Chandler was formerly Wiltshire's local studies librarian, but has worked freelance for many years, writing, lecturing, editing and undertaking historical research. The author of various books about the county and on regional and landscape history topics, he now publishes local books, as *Hobnob Press*.

Chris Cole Born in the flat landscape of the Cambridgeshire fenland, Chris is more than familiar with the type of river floodplain that is a prominent feature of his walk in this collection. After moving south some years ago, he now devotes his time to writing and photography, producing countryside and local history articles for magazines such as *Wiltshire Life*.

Victoria Coombes has lived in the Salisbury area since 1986. She is the author of *Take the Footpath, 40 walks in the Salisbury Area*, and has written for *Wiltshire Life*. A country lover, Victoria says her day is made if she spots a kingfisher on the River Bourne near her home.

Nick Cowen grew up in the Wylye Valley, gained a Fine Art Degree in South Wales and for the last 12 years has been working as the Rights of Way Warden for South Wiltshire. Through his work Nick has become very familiar with even the remotest parts of his area and hopes to illustrate and write more about this wonderfully rich and varied landscape. He now lives in Wilton with his family.

Isobel Geddes lives in Keevil, between Trowbridge and Devizes. A geologist by background, she is also a Blue Badge Guide qualified for south-west England. She has written a book on Wiltshire's geology and landscapes, so has explored the county thoroughly.

Roger Jones, with his wife, has run the Ex Libris Bookshop in Bradford on Avon since 1980. Under his imprint, Ex Libris Press, he has published more than 100 books on Wiltshire and the West Country, country life and the Channel Islands, including a number of walking guides, some of which he has compiled himself.

Julian Richards, before he became well known as the presenter of television and radio programmes (including *Meet the Ancestors, Blood of the Vikings* and *Mapping the Town*) worked as an archaeologist in Wiltshire. His speciality is prehistoric England, and he has researched, written and lectured extensively on Stonehenge and its landscape. He lives in Shaftesbury.

Rex Sawyer was for 18 years headmaster of the middle and secondary schools at Wilton and a local magistrate. Since coming to Wiltshire in 1972 Rex and his wife Sheila have led walks regularly for the South Wilts Ramblers Association. They have lived at Bowerchalke and now Tisbury, and Rex has written seven books on south Wiltshire, including (most recently) a history of Imber.

Nigel Vile lives in Bradford-on-Avon and teaches at King Edward's School in Bath. As well as a weekly walking feature for *The Bath Chronicle*, he is the Wiltshire contributor for *Country Walking* magazine. He is the author of several walking guidebooks, including *Family Walks in the Downs and Vales of Wiltshire* (Scarthin Books) and *Short Walks from Wiltshire Pubs* (Countryside Books).

Ken Watts is a native of Wiltshire, a retired architect and an experienced walker who has studied the county's history and associations for the past forty years. He has led many guided walks for various organisations and was a Ridgeway Warden. He has published extensively on the county, and his major study of Wiltshire personalities, *Figures in a Wiltshire Scene*, is about to appear.